The text of *Fighter Pilot* was written by Duff Hart-Davis, based largely on the research and the hundreds of interviews by Colin Strong over a period of three and a half years spent following the student-pilots through training. As Producer of the television series, Colin Strong was able to gain a unique insight into the methods of the RAF, even going to the lengths of learning to fly a Jet Provost trainer, eventually going solo. A member of the BBC staff, he worked as a studio director on many Light Entertainment series, including *The Old Grey Whistle Test*, *Till Death Us Do Part* and *Parkinson*, before becoming a documentary producer.

As feature writer for the *Sunday Telegraph*, Duff Hart-Davis has reported from many parts of the world, and has flown as an observer on several fast-jet sorties with the RAF, including Lightning, Phantom, Jaguar, Buccaneer, Hawk and Hunter. He has written six adventure novels, notably *The Heights of Rimring*, and is the author of the celebrated biography of Peter Fleming.

D1550246

Colin Strong and
Duff Hart-Davis

Fighter Pilot

Futura
Macdonald & Co
London & Sydney

British Broadcasting Corporation

A Futura Book

First published in Great Britain in 1981 by
Queen Anne Press, a Division of Macdonald & Co
(Publishers) Ltd

and

British Broadcasting Corporation
35 Marylebone High Street
London W1M 4AA

This edition published simultaneously by Futura
Publications and British Broadcasting Corporation 1982

ISBN 0 7088 2193 6 (Futura)
ISBN 0 563 20135 5 (British Broadcasting Corporation)

Filmset, printed and bound in Great Britain by
Hazell Watson & Viney Ltd, Aylesbury, Bucks

Futura Publications
A Division of
Macdonald & Co (Publishers) Ltd
Maxwell House
74 Worship Street
London EC2A 2EN

Contents

Foreword

AIR CHIEF MARSHAL
SIR KEITH WILLIAMSON, KCB, AFC, RAF
Air Officer Commanding-in-Chief
Royal Air Force Strike Command

The record of the Royal Air Force in war bears eloquent witness to the high standards required of the young men who so proudly wear the RAF pilot's brevet on their uniforms. These standards were set in the early days of the life of the Royal Air Force when, as a matter of policy, we attempted to establish a central core of expertise in the air in peace-time on which we would be able to build an expanded Royal Air Force should the need ever arise.

Since those early days, military aircraft have become far more expensive and sophisticated and the required training standards are, as a consequence, now higher than they have ever been. I believe that the standing of the Royal Air Force today in the aviation world is evidence enough that our modern generation of pilots are in fact meeting those standards.

But training our pilots to this level is a long and expensive process and it is this process that Colin Strong has endeavoured to portray in his film series for the BBC. In doing this Mr Strong followed the progress of six prospective Royal Air Force pilots as they moved through the RAF's training machine. Over a period of three and a half years he recorded their successes and failures from the Aircrew Selection

Centre to the front line cockpit. It was a unique opportunity to portray a worm's eye view of the process and Colin Strong went to extraordinary lengths to ensure that the view that emerged was both frank and balanced. Indeed, in an effort to ensure that he properly understood the problems facing student pilots, Mr Strong was, at his own request, given some flying instruction at the end of which he flew a solo sortie in the Jet Provost. He was thus very well equipped to be able impartially to record how this particular group of young men coped with the problems they faced.

The result is a fascinating, well-balanced, lively and human story of the way we train our young men for our particular military skill. This account has been written jointly by Duff Hart-Davis and Colin Strong and I am sure that anyone with an interest in flying, whether military or civil, will find it utterly engrossing.

Introduction

The idea for this book was born in 1978, when the Royal Air Force and the British Broadcasting Corporation agreed to work together on a documentary film about the training of fast-jet pilots. The RAF, already short of pilots and worried by the poor level of recruiting, welcomed the prospect of any publicity that the film might bring; and thanks to the wholehearted co-operation of the Service, the BBC television producer Colin Strong was able to make a uniquely comprehensive record of the three-year training process.

From the first day, when hopeful candidates reported to the Officers and Aircrew Selection Centre at Biggin Hill, he followed one ever-diminishing band of student-pilots through Officer Cadet Training at Henlow, Basic Flying Training at Linton-on-Ouse, Advanced Flying Training at Valley, the Tactical Weapons Unit at Brawdy and the Buccaneer Operational Conversion Unit at Honington to XV Squadron at Laarbruch, in West Germany. The series of programmes first shown by the BBC in the autumn of 1981 portrays the RAF in action with a degree of detail and fidelity never captured before.

Only a select few pass out to fly fast jets – the Tornado, Harrier, Jaguar, Phantom, Lightning or Buccaneer. Those who fail narrowly may 'go multi-engine' – that is, fly less-demanding aeroplanes such as Hercules transports, Nimrod maritime surveillance jets, or Canberra photo-reconnaissance aircraft. Others fly helicopters, and others again opt to become navigators instead of pilots.

Here it should be emphasized that in the past twenty years RAF, and indeed NATO, aerial-warfare policy has gone through a fundamental change. Until the early 1960s the RAF maintained what might be called a traditional bombing capability: Vulcan crews were trained to bomb from high altitude as well as from low level. Then, with the development of intercontinental ballistic weapons on the one hand, and the continual improvement of radar defences and surface-to-air missiles on the other, high-level bombing became obsolete. The only way in which an attacking aeroplane could reach its target – the new theory went – was by going in at extremely low level – at or below 250 feet – beneath the height at which radar can maintain an effective watch.

Of the fast jets now in RAF service, the Lightnings and Phantoms are used for air defence, their role being to intercept attackers at any height from sea level to 60,000 feet or above. The rest – Harriers, Jaguars and Buccaneers – are all designed for low-level operation; their pilots are trained to fly down to 250 feet at speeds up to 550 knots, or 640 mph. (For conversion purposes, 6 knots=7 mph.) The Tornado, now starting to enter RAF service, is a multi-role aircraft whose variable geometry (in other words, swing-wing system) enables it to do both jobs. As the 386 Tornados ordered by the RAF come into service during the 1980s, they will gradually replace nearly all the other types of fast jet.

An aeroplane flying at 550 knots travels nearly 1000 feet per second – the length of four football pitches in a count of one. At that speed the workload on the pilot is extremely heavy. Not only must his pure flying skill be of the highest order. He also needs to be tough, both mentally and physically. He must be able to deal with problems instantly, as they arise: to make quick decisions and put them behind him without worrying. His life depends on his determination and tenacity, on

10

his ability to keep going at high speed down in that fraught but friendly airspace at or below 250 feet where the enemy radars cannot get him.

Obviously the workload is heaviest in single-seat aeroplanes (Harriers, Jaguars and Lightnings), for the pilot has to do his own navigating and weapon-handling, besides actually flying. (The Harrier, with its vertical-take-off capability, is the most demanding of all.) But even when reinforced by a navigator (as in Tornados, Phantoms and Buccaneers) the pilot must still be a man of formidable skills. Particularly at low level, he cannot afford to make mistakes: every second, the lives of himself and his partner are in his hands.

His training must therefore also be formidable – and it is his exacting three-year schedule that this book follows. By the time he passes out on to an operational squadron, he has cost the taxpayer an enormous sum. In 1978 it was reckoned at £1 million; now it is at least £1.7 million. This, then, is a portrait of million-pound pilots in the making.

Glossary

The Battle of Britain slang ('wizard prang', and so on) with which many people still associate the RAF has largely disappeared. But it has been replaced by a new form of private language which strikes outsiders as strange and baffling, not least because it contains so many initials and abbreviations.

These reflect the ever-increasing complexity of RAF training and equipment. The technical knowledge needed by air-crew today is immeasurably greater than that on which their predecessors could get by a generation ago, and the number of technical terms in use is correspondingly larger. The expressions listed here are all part of everyday speech, used and understood without explanation.

ADIZ air defence identification zone

AGL above ground level

AOA angle of attack

ASAP as soon as possible

ASL above sea level

ATAF allied tactical air force

ATC air traffic control

AUW all-up weight

Bingos radio calls to report fuel states

Bogie strange or enemy aircraft

Bunt to push the nose down, go into a dive

Buster codeword to accelerate: enemy aircraft sighted

Bx bombs

CAP combat air patrol

CASS centralized audio selection system

CBU cluster bomb unit

CI chief instructor

Clangers warning system in cockpit

CPT cockpit procedures trainer

Creamy outstanding student creamed off after advanced flying training to become a flying instructor

DCO duty carried out

ECM electronic counter-measures

EHT elementary handling test

EW electronic warfare

Eyeball (verb) to judge by eye

Fam Trip familiarization flight (in new aircraft)

FHT final handling test

Finals the final approach to the runway

FNT final navigation test

FOD foreign object damage. As noun, screw, nut etc. that gets into engine or control system

Fodded (engine) damaged by foreign object

Fox codeword for a hit in air-to-air combat. Fox One is a head-on hit; Fox Two, stern with missile; Fox Three, gunnery

FRA first-run attack

FRCs flight reference cards, listing all actions required for aircraft operation, including emergencies. Invariably carried by a pilot in the air.

g gravity, the force of gravity. Used to measure the tightness of a turn. At four g, for example, everything feels four times its normal weight.

GA ground attack

GCA ground-controlled approach

GCI ground-controlled intercept

Gotcha snatch raid in which air-crew are taken for unannounced survival training

GPI ground position indicator

Hack code word to start manoeuvre in the air. As verb, to succeed, manage something, get what one wants

Hairy former NCO, generally an old sweat, training to become an officer

HAS hardened aircraft shelter

HEFOE mnemonic for hydraulics, electrics, fuel, oxygen, engine – checks done in the air

Hot Poop latest information

HUD head-up display

IAS indicated air speed

14

IFF identification – friend or foe

ILS instrument landing system

Indulge take free, non-duty passage in RAF transport aircraft

IP initial point, from which the target run is made in air-to-ground attack

JPT jet pipe temperature

LOA line of approach

LSJ life-saving jacket

Mahogany Bombers the desks which office-bound pilots fly

MDC miniature detonating cord – an explosive device that shatters the canopy if the crew has to eject

MSD minimum safe distance

Mud Movers nickname, sometimes derisive, for ground-attack pilots

NB not below

NBC nuclear, biological and chemical

Ninety ninety-degree turn

NOTAM notice to airman

OCU operational conversion unit

PBF pilot briefing facility

PEC personal equipment connector

Pickle to release bombs or rockets

Pigs mistakes, mess, hash – to make a pigs

Pipper aiming dot in centre of gunsight

POB persons on board (sometimes SOB, souls on board)

POL petrol, oil and lubricants

Pole control column

PSP personal survival pack, containing dinghy etc.

PUP pull-up point

PVR premature voluntary retirement

QFI qualified flying instructor

QRA or Q quick-reaction alert, maintained by crews at instant readiness to fly

QWI qualified weapons instructor

Recover return to base after a sortie

Recovery the return to base

Retread aviator returned to flying duties after ground tour

Roller practice touch-down immediately followed by another take-off

RT radio transmission

RWR radar warning receiver

Rx rockets

SAM surface-to-air missile

SAP simulated attack profile

SAR search and rescue

Shackle scissors manoeuvre in which two aeroplanes, or two pairs of aeroplanes, change sides

Six six o'clock, or tail – the area straight behind an aeroplane

Sixty sixty-degree turn

SOP standard operating procedure

Squawk radar identification signal

Stores bombs, rockets, fuel tanks or special equipment pods slung under an aircraft's fuselage or wings

SWO station warrant officer

SWP standard warning panel

Taceval tactical evaluation exercise

TGT turbine gas temperature

Tits-up unserviceable, out of action (used of aeroplanes, cars, plans, people: tits-up on the runway)

Two-ship formation of two aeroplanes (cf. four-ship)

VAs vital actions (pre-landing checks)

VFR visual flying rules

VRIAB visual run-in and break

Wanker (fig.) universal derogatory term for someone not trusted or thought little of

WCP weapon control panel

Wx weapons

To avoid mis-hearings and ambiguities, the RAF uses the phonetic alphabet given below.

A Alpha	N November
B Bravo	O Oscar
C Charlie	P Papa
D Delta	Q Quebec
E Echo	R Romeo
F Foxtrot	S Sierra
G Golf	T Tango
H Hotel	U Uniform
I India	V Victor
J Juliet	W Whisky
K Kilo	X X-ray
L Lima	Y Yankee
M Mike	Z Zulu

In speech 'zero' is always used for 'nought', and composite numbers are given in separate digits: 2050, for instance, would be 'two zero five zero' rather than 'two thousand and fifty'.

1.

Buster! Buster!

'Today's aim is a Two-ATAF lo-lo. We'll go straight up to Nordhorn as a four-ship, and drop some bombs in a co-ordinated FRA. A Phantom bounce has been arranged for when we come off the range, so we may have that to contend with. Then we'll do three SAP's – a SAM site, an airfield and a POL site – and then we'll come home.'

We are in the Pilot Briefing Facility of 16 Squadron at RAF Laarbruch, in the north-west corner of Germany, just inside the Dutch border. Laarbruch is one of the RAF's four bases in Germany and houses two squadrons of Buccaneer long-range fighter bombers, besides a squadron of photo-reconnaissance Jaguars.

Everything one can see emphasizes the fact that this is a front-line station. The airfield is defended by ground-to-air missiles, camouflaged towers and pill-boxes, and miles of coiled barbed wire. The PBF – commonly known as 'the hard' – is a windowless reinforced building designed to withstand a near-miss from a 1000-lb bomb. It is equipped with an elaborate system of air-conditioning which will protect its inmates from nuclear fallout or from chemical and biological attacks. Inside, the walls are plastered with photographs and descriptions of Warsaw Pact aircraft, tanks, guns and equipment.

In the event of war in Europe, 16 Squadron, as part of NATO, would be tasked to attack targets anywhere within range of its S Mk 2B Buccaneers. The formidable armament which these low-level strike aircraft carry includes nuclear bombs, known to the crews as 'buckets of instant sunshine'.

Because they were formed at St Omer in 1915, 16 Squadron are traditionally known as The Saints. But they are not in Germany to fly mercy missions. Today the briefing officer is Flt Lt Ron Trinder, who is going to lead the formation. Translated, his opening summary means that the aim is to carry out a typical Second Tactical Airforce low-level training sortie against targets in northern Germany. The formation of four Buccaneers will go first to the bombing range at Nordhorn, where it will put in a co-ordinated first-run attack. Our route has been passed to one of the Phantom squadrons at RAF Wildenrath. If the fighters want someone on whom to practise, they can come and bounce us – that is, make a mock attack and try to drive us off track. After that, we will do three simulated attack profiles – attacks with imaginary weapons – against real targets in the field: the first a surface-to-air missile site, the second an airfield, and the third a petrol and oil depot. No real weapons will be used on the field targets, but cine-film will be shot through the gun-sights so that the accuracy of the attacks can be analysed afterwards.

Eight people are present at the briefing: four pilots, three navigators, and myself. I am to fly with the Squadron Commander, Wing Commander Peter Norriss. Everyone is wearing drab green flying overalls with the owner's name emblazoned on the chest. The faces are not as young as I expected: the men are in their late twenties or early thirties. Peter Norris himself is lean and dark, with an angular chin and penetrating pale-blue eyes.

The atmosphere is taut and expectant, the briefing to match: staccato, thorough, and so packed with initials and numbers as to be scarcely comprehensible to a civilian. No relevant fact is missed out, for in this kind of low-level sortie meticulous preparation is essential. A pilot flying at 250 feet or below, at speeds

20

up to 600 mph, has very little time to make decisions; so the more decisions he can put behind him before he even takes off, the easier his task will be.

Here on the ground, Flt Lt Trinder refers to everyone by his Christian name, except for the Squadron Commander whom he addresses as 'Boss' and refers to as 'the Boss'. But in the air everyone will become a number. The formation's call-sign will be 1302 Green Section, the leader Green One, ourselves Green Two, the others Green Three and Green Four.

Each aircrew member has marked himself up a map depicting the entire route. On the 1:500,000 map (generally known as the 'half-mill') every turning-point and heading has been marked in bold black ink. For each of the SAPs a sheet of the large scale 1:50,000 map has been similarly drawn up, but in greater detail.

Quickly but carefully, Flt Lt Trinder runs through every phase of the sortie. We will check in (from the aircraft) at fifteen minutes past the next hour (11 a.m. local time) for take-off eight minutes later. We will take off in ten-second stream from runway one-zero and climb out in a standard departure. Our height throughout the sortie will be 500 feet, except when we are in designated low-flying areas, where we will descend to the permitted limit of 250 feet. Over the Nordhorn range we are allowed down to 150 feet. The weather in our area is 'blue' – clear skies – but on some parts of the route it is 'red' – cloud down to 200 feet – so that some parts of the plan may have to be omitted.

Our route to Nordhorn will take us out past a power-station known as 'Smokies' to the Dummer See, a large lake; and then sharp left up to the Meppen army training area and the range. Already our slot in the range programme has been booked, so we must arrive there within a few seconds of the allotted time. As we approach, we will switch to stud 10 on the radio and announce ourselves to the range controller. Then we will run in on a heading of 171 degrees, accelerating to 500 knots and descending to 150 feet. The leader will

21

do a lay-down attack (dropping his bombs without pulling up). We, Number Two, will go through 'hanging on his wing', to watch his performance. Numbers Three and Four will come through as a pair ten seconds later, Three pulling up to do a toss attack (a kind of lob) on one target, and Four bunting (going into a shallow dive) to attack the other.

Off the range, we will resume our cruising speed and fly a pattern of zigzags – long-sided, 180-degree turns – to give the Phantoms a chance to pick us up, if they are about, then fly on to the first SAP, against the missile site. For this, a salient feature has been chosen from the map to be the initial point, or IP, from which the final run to the target starts. In this case the IP is a factory just east of a small town: it is picked out on the map with a thick black square. Thereafter, another thick line marks the track to the pull-up point, where the aircraft will climb briefly before they tip in and dive right-handed at the target.

Across the track, like rungs on a ladder, are lateral bars marking where an aeroplane travelling at the attack speed of 520 knots will be at ten-second intervals. Ten, twenty, thirty, forty – the figures have a seductive simplicity. Also marked on the map is the heading to the pull-up point – 343 degrees – and information about the setting needed on the weapon-sights. The target itself is highlighted by a boldly drawn triangle.

As with the attack on the range, the orders are absolutely precise: 'The aim is to put all four aircraft through as quickly as possible. The leader – that's me – will be bunting with CBUs /cluster bomb units/ to mark the target, which is not easy to see. Everyone else will simulate dropping thousand-pounders. Two, you'll be on my left, slightly swept, over the target with a minimum spacing of five seconds. Three and four, you'll come through as a pair thirty seconds later. Off the target, continue right on to a heading of 106 degrees. The installation isn't very big, but I want to see film of the pipper buried in the bottom of it . . .'

No detail of the sortie is left to chance. Even the tactics in the event of a bounce are spelt out: 'Normal rules of combat training will apply. 500 feet is the minimum height for manoeuvring. No vertical jinking. Minimum speed, 300 knots. Minimum range, 300 yards. No head-on attacks. If we don't like it, we'll call "Stop, stop, stop," and waggle our wings.'

At the end, the leader quickly sums up: 'So there we are. Our primary formation throughout will be Card. Go into pairs trail if the weather gets bad. On the EW side, I want minimum chat – hazards and threats only please. Listen out on your RWR and if you get any threats, call them early. Let's get the team looking at them quickly. Keep a good look out – I don't want anyone getting in on our six before we see him.

'Coming back here – standard visual run in and break. Standard defensive battle breaking downwind to land. Emergencies will be SOP, If *you* get an emergency, Boss, we'll give you all the help we can. If you need escorting, we'll take you.'

The briefing lasts half an hour. By the end of it my nerves are fully on edge. There is just time for a last-minute visit to the lavatory, something rendered less simple than usual by my g-suit – a pair of futuristic trousers honeycombed by air-channels which inflate hard against stomach, thighs, and calves when the aeroplane starts pulling g.

I collect my gloves, bonedome helmet, and life-saving jacket. Outside, it is a lovely May morning, with bright sunshine and a soft breeze. Blackbirds are singing all round the camp; but everything else is menacingly warlike. On this base no aircraft stand parked in rows out on the tarmac to make an easy target. The only things in sight by the ends of the runway are the batteries of surface-to-air missiles, bristling like lances raised to the sky. The aeroplanes

23

are all tucked away out of sight in hardened shelters dispersed among the pine woods.

A minibus takes us out to HAS Five, nestling in the trees at the end of its own concrete strip. The steel doors are open. In the centre of the arched shelter stands one Buccaneer, big and heavy at close quarters, camouflaged grey and green. The aircraft has been nicknamed 'the flying banana', but its ungainly appearance belies its low-level performance, which is still second to none.

Under its nose stands a red-and-yellow notice saying AIRCRAFT ARMED. Another notice is hung on each of the ladders going up ten feet to the front and back cockpits: AIRCRAFT ARMED, AIRCRAFT ARMED. I climb the back ladder and ease myself down on to the navigator's seat. Compared with the cockpits of some other fast jets, this one is spacious. Even so, to a civilian it seems horribly small. My knees are jammed up against the underneath of the central instrument panel, and all around me is a stupefying array of dials and switches. Except on the seat, which itself is pretty hard, there is no padding at all. The decor is entirely of black paint, metal scraped bare, sharp edges, dials, switches.

I have already had instruction in the hangar, but still I need help strapping in. A volunteer from 16 Squadron gives me a hand. The first thing to do is to push home the personal equipment connector, down by my right thigh. This connects up the oxygen supply and the pressure system that inflates the g-suit. Next is the lanyard attached to the personal survival pack containing the dinghy, down on the left. Next the leg restraints – thick nylon cords that loop round each lower leg and plug into sockets. Should I have to eject, the seat mechanism will automatically draw tight the restraints which will pull my legs in under me, so that they do not flail about and get broken. Another important detail is to dial my all-up weight, 230 lbs, into the little window down on my left.

Next, the harness. One pair of straps comes up

between my legs, another in from outside my hips, and two pairs down over my shoulders. All lock into a central socket over my crutch. As soon as I have the ends clicked home, I wriggle and jerk everything tight until, like the tentacles of an octopus, the straps have me clamped into the back of the seat. Now it is difficult to move my trunk at all.

My helper hands me down the bonedome. I pull it on, fighting to get my ears unfolded inside the inner cradle, which has been adjusted by two sets of screws to fit as snugly as possible. By the time I have connected the oxygen and radio leads, and snapped down the lever of the black-rubber oxygen mask, I am in another world.

No one who suffers from claustrophobia should try this kind of flying. Within a few seconds I am feeling hot and boxed-in, constricted by the grip of the harness and the weight of the flying kit. The only comfortable things I am wearing are the gloves, which are made of the finest soft white leather. The high quality is not an extravagance, but a practical necessity, with two particular advantages: the fine leather gives the wearer excellent feel, and – more sinister – it is fire-retardant.

The seats in a Buccaneer are slightly offset, the navigator's to the right and the pilot's to the left. Thus, looking forward over the top of the instrument panel, I can see the back of the pilot's helmet and over his right shoulder through the windshield, down towards the nose.

There in the front seat the Boss is busy with his pre-start-up checks. When he switches on the power my instruments are lit up by a bright red glow. Somehow I must remember the few things that, passenger though I am, I have been trained to do. One such task is to turn on and off the various fuel-pump switches when the pilot asks. With them, down on my left, are the compass, air-speed indicator and altimeter.

All across my front is a bank of weapons switches, which I shall not be touching. By my left knee is the radar display, and by my right the radar warning receiver, which will alert us both visually and audibly if we come within range of enemy radar. In the same area is the GPI (ground position indicator) and corrector unit, both of which help tell a trained navigator where he is. Further down to the right is the CASS box, with switches that control the radio and intercom. Also down there is the IFF, the instrument which produces the 'squawk' – a radar beacon used specifically for identifying our aircraft to receivers on the ground. This, too, is something that I may have to reset during the sortie. The instruments mentioned are only a few of the dozens that crowd the cockpit.

I struggle to come to terms with the feeling of being trapped. It is difficult even to look down, because the coiled snout of the oxygen mask is in the way. Every sound of respiration is caught and magnified by the microphone built into the mask: *hiss*, in; *rasp*, out. I watch the doll's-eye indicator on the instrument panel, blinking white on the in-breath, black on the out, and try to slow it down.

A sudden whooping, shrieking noise blasts through the intercom as the Boss tests the clangers – the alarm system. 'Just checking that the machine is in one piece,' he says casually. His voice is loud and clear in my headphones. But as soon as he uses the Palouste air-starter to start the engines, the noise becomes so deafening that I can hardly hear him.

Thunder comes roaring round the concrete vault of the shelter and blasts in through the bonedome. My helper is still delving head-down into the depths of the cockpit to pull out the safety-pins whose removal arms the ejector seat. One is down beneath me, another behind my left shoulder. At last all the red-tagged pins are stowed in their proper holders, six behind the Boss's right shoulder and five on my right.

The noise is indescribable. Hot gusts of kerosene exhaust come belting down into the cockpit from behind. The ground crew, in ear-protectors, are making vigorous hand signals to confirm that the flaps and airbrakes are working. Through the hurricane I hear everybody coming up on the radio: 'Green One, check in.' 'Green Two.' 'Three.' 'Four.' The Boss tells me to keep my hands clear as he closes the canopy. The perspex comes forward and locks into place with a thump, cutting out the worst of the noise. At last we roll out into the sunlight, and the roar is left behind us.

As we taxi the Boss runs through the emergency procedures: 'If we have to abort the take-off, I'll drop the hook and engage the cable . . . After take-off, if you hear me calling "Eject, eject!" grasp the handle between your legs, get your head well back and go straight away. It's quite a hard pull, but by then you'll be feeling so strong you won't notice it.'

At the end of the runway the formation quickly lines up. Of the first pair, the leader is on the left, ourselves on the right. At the last moment the Boss asks me to check that the visor on my helmet is down, my harness tight and locked. A brief pause, and then the leader's white-gloved hand comes up. Suddenly his aeroplane is rolling. Away it goes down the runway, spurting black trails from its engines. The Boss opens our own throttles. The roar at my back begins to build. The aeroplane is trembling. 'Power coming up,' he says tensely. 'Five . . . eight, nine – *and we're going.*'

Brakes off. We jump forward, then accelerate smoothly. The Boss keeps up a running commentary as the speed builds. At 179 knots we are airborne. We climb straight ahead and wheel left. In a few more seconds we are at 500 feet and 420 knots, our transit speed. At once we are established in standard defensive battle formation, some 1500 yards from our leader and level with him. A layman might think that the little black dart, slicing along out there far on our left, was nothing to do with us, but in fact the formation is vital for our mutual protection. The most valuable quarter of each aeroplane is its 'six' – the area straight behind it, which the crew cannot see. If a bogie decides to attack, it is probably from there that he will come. Therefore the prime duty of every crew in formation is to watch its partner's six.

Almost at once we pass over the Rhine, wide and brown and sluggish. At first our passage is very smooth. The Buccaneer is beautifully stable, hence its excellence as a weapons platform. The neat, flat, fenceless fields of the great North German plain go slipping by easily beneath us. I am just beginning to enjoy the trip when everything goes berserk. Without warning the world tilts on edge. Suddenly the land-sky division is vertical instead of horizontal. It takes me a second to realize that it is our aeroplane, not the universe, which has rolled over. My head and arms have turned to lead. The g-suit has snatched at my stomach and legs and is gripping me with a prodigious squeeze. Belatedly I realize that this is the first of the pre-planned turns.

Forcing myself to look out, I see that the green and brown fields are straight beneath my left shoulder, geometrically neat and rectangular. The g-forces tell me that I am upright and the rest of the world at fault. But just as I start to get myself together we roll out on to our new heading and the pressure vanishes.

The turn leaves me gasping. But I see from the map that we are coming to the first of the low-flying areas. Sure enough, we start letting down. At 250 feet the ground slides by a great deal faster. The slender spires of the village churches seem to reach halfway to us, the tops of electricity pylons to pass just beneath our wings. I know from the map that another turn must be imminent – a right-hander. I start bracing myself for it. Looking forward, I notice that the Boss's head is constantly moving as he twists back and forth, eyeballing the sky for bogies. For a moment he looks steadily out to the left. 'He'll want to turn any minute now,' he says. 'Here he comes.'

Being on the outside this time, the leader has initiated the turn. The little black dart in the distance has canted over, silhouetting itself against the sky, its back towards us. For a few seconds it seems to keep pace with us, then suddenly it starts falling behind as it heads in our direction. With a sickening flip our right wing goes down as we, too, start pulling round. Again the g-pressure slams me into the seat. Quite by chance I catch a thrilling glimpse of our partner as he hurtles across above us. Before I have come to terms with myself, we are level again on our new heading, back in formation, having switched sides.

I don't feel at all confident of surviving this sort of thing for long. Yet these gentle turns – I soon find – are nothing compared with what lies ahead. So far we have flown in radio silence. But now over the air comes the sharp call, 'Buster! Buster!'

I feel us accelerate. Dimly I remember that 'Buster!' is the emergency call to warn that a bogie is attacking. The needle of the air-speed indicator goes climbing through the 500-knots mark. With my right hand I reach down for the CASS box and jab the button to give me an audio signal from the radar warning receiver. Sure enough, among the myriad twitterings and scrapings of the background mush there is the sharp, giveaway tone: *ee-ee, ee-ee*. A bogie has us: a sector-scan radar has seen us.

Were I able to work the visual warning equipment, I would be able to tell what sector he is in. But I can't – and in any case it is too late, for life has suddenly become so violent that I am no longer capable of rational conduct. We have gone into a series of desperate turns, hard to the left, hard to the right. The g-forces heave at me remorselessly, right, left, up, down. I can feel the skin of my face being dragged down. I can hardly get my right hand up off my knee. Even my eyeballs are heavy as lead and will no longer do what I want them to do, so that I am as good as blind.

Now we are climbing. Or are we descending? I can't be sure – and, what's worse, I can't bring myself to care, for my stomach has begun to throw some manoeuvres of its own and seems to have come three-quarters of the way up to my mouth.

My earphones are full of quick-fire reports as the crews direct each other in the fight: 'He's high in your five, heading right . . . He's low in your seven . . .' I cannot pay attention to them. My immediate concern is that I am going to be sick into my oxygen mask. I start trying to take the mask off. Then I change my mind – maybe there is nothing but air to come up. Still I am straining every muscle to fight the pull of the g.

We are manoeuvring as hard as ever. Suddenly I *do* hear something clearly: the Boss is calling, 'Fox Two! Camera! Can you hear me? Camera!' With an all-out effort I force myself to find the button, back on my left, and jam it in. More commands ricochet back and forth through the air. The Boss calls something about retard defence. But for me, life has become a question of somehow holding out until – pray God – we go straight and level again.

At last the pressure eases. Our speed comes back to 420. I can get my head upright and see out again. The relief is unbelievable, and none too soon in coming for I am in an absolute muck sweat. The whole of my torso is soaked, and the oxygen mask is sliding greasily around my face. I discipline myself to calm down: imagine what it would be like if you actually had to *do* something, I tell myself, instead of just sitting there.

Not until later, after we have landed, do I find out what all the fuss was about. For the moment, we are already in touch with the range at Nordhorn and running in for the first of the FRAs.

We pass the two check-points, X-ray and Yankee. The needle of the air-speed indicator goes smoothly up again to 500 knots. Down we go, down, down, down until the tops of the fir trees below are whizzing past in a solid blur. We are covering 950 feet per second. At 150 feet the sensation of speed is electrifying, but still the ride is rock-steady. The Boss eases us in until we are only a few hundred yards behind the leader, and just to one side of his track. We should have a perfect view of his bombs.

The fir trees give way to a bare moor of heather and peat. The target is in sight – a bus conveniently painted red and white. Running in, we are so close to the leader that we can see the 4-lb practice bombs fall away from under his wings. Flashes and puffs of smoke erupt from right beside the bus. Direct hit! In an instant we ourselves are past the target and pulling hard up to the left. Behind us, thirty seconds later, Three and Four come tearing through. The range controller calls up on the radio to confirm the positions of the bombs. The first attack went in within four seconds of the time set for it before take-off.

Three more times we come round and go scorching over the woods and the moor. Thank God I do not feel frightened, because if I did, I should be half-mad by now. There is no escape from this rocketing capsule. At 500 knots and 150 feet, life itself seems to accelerate into a different gear. One mistake by the pilot and we would instantly be blown into smithereens. But this is the height and speed at which the Buccaneers would have to fly a war mission to give themselves a chance of getting in beneath the enemy radar – scraping their backsides along the ground (as one pilot puts it) all the way to the target. My admiration for the professionalism of the crews increases by the minute.

As we clear the range for the last time the leader calls the controller and thanks him for his help. 'You're welcome,' comes the answer. 'Good day to you, and good hunting.' We make a wide turn to resume defensive formation and start on the series of dog-legs originally designed to let the Phantoms have a go at us. But here there *are* no Phantoms: the bogie who tapped us before – crafty sod – was not in the area in which we expected him.

In a few minutes we are heading north to the first of the SAPs. Abeam of the village of Friesoythe we start to accelerate again – time for the large-scale map.

There, on the clear, light background, everything looks deceptively simple. All we need do is follow the thick black line from IP to target.

The real thing is not so easy. By the time we reach the IP we are doing 520 knots. Our heading is 343, as it should be, but maybe we are a bit left of track. A proper navigator would now give the pilot continuous help with the identification of the vital features on the ground; but because I am a useless passenger, we go slightly astray. At twelve seconds we pass over the canal, and at thirty-five we clear the village of Remels. Are we too far to the left? Where is the wooded hill at the pull-up point? At forty-five seconds we pull up anyway and tip right-handed into a shallow dive, but the SAM site is not on the nose, as it should be. We go boring down towards a patch of empty country.

The Boss calls: 'There it is – on the left!' We pull up, turn hard, tip-in again. This time, as we go down the dive, the dome of the missile site's radar installation is dead on the nose.

By the time we roll out on to our next heading, the rest of the formation has left us behind. To catch them up we keep going at 500 knots instead of throttling back to 420. The weather has deteriorated: the haze has thickened, and the horizon is a murky blur. We hammer into it, searching the sky for signs of our comrades. At last we pick up a speck at eleven o'clock, ahead and to the left, then another. They are Buccaneers, but which is which? The Boss puts out a quick call on the radio: 'Green leader, waggle.' One of the specks instantly flicks its wings, and we slide back into position.

We cross another big river, the Weser. Bremerhaven is to our left, Bremen to our right. The estuary is spiky with cranes, the river laden with cargo vessels. Turning south-east, we leave Hamburg on our left. Now we are in the buffer zone that cushions the frontier: the air defence identification zone – the no-man's-land along the border – is only a few miles to our left. We are within three minutes' flying time of East Germany. It is odd to reflect that British and American bombers flew over this territory – not at 500 feet, but at more like 25,000 – day after day, night after night, nearly forty years ago.

The target for the second SAP is a small airfield. As we approach it our leader calls up the control tower and confirms that we have permission for a couple of low passes. This time there is no problem with the run-in. The IP, a sports stadium, stands out perfectly and I hit the button of the stop-watch dead above it. Everything looks good: our speed is 520 knots, our heading 249. At sixteen seconds we cross the railroad junction, at twenty seconds the power lines. At twenty-eight we pull up right-handed over the neck of the woods, soar for a few seconds, tip in and dive. The neat pattern of runways and hangars comes hurtling up towards us, growing as if I had it in a zoom lens. I wait till we are almost on top of it and jab the button of our camera. For a second or two we hold our trajectory, then pull violently up and away.

The final attack goes almost as well. This time the general position of the target is obvious from miles away because it lies at the foot of a ridge. Coming down from the north, we approach the hills at right-angles: the petrol and oil tanks must be just this side of them. As always, the job of actually picking them out is not so easy.

This time there is a pre-IP – a village – which should lead us to the IP itself, a factory. But here the trouble begins. The country is flat and featureless. There are roads leading in all directions, not easy to distinguish from each other, and the IP does not stand out as much as we had hoped. Nevertheless, I hit my stop-watch. Our heading is correct: 156. Ten seconds, twenty, thirty: there should be some woods, some houses, more woods. Nothing seems quite right, but there is no time to worry. At forty-one seconds we pull up and tip in right-handed. In the valley ahead is a big canal, at right-angles to our track. The complex is beyond it. We have them – fat, white cylindrical tanks, just right for a shower of cluster-bombs. We go down the dive dead at them: again, they grow at a mesmerizing speed. I give them a blast with the camera just before we pull up. Then, in a flash, they are gone beneath us, and we are turning away to avoid the helicopter base marked on our maps with a capital H in a circle.

We climb out over the line of wooded hills and set course for home, once again in defensive battle. One more turn, and we are back in Low Flying Area No 2, crossing our outward track to run in to Laarbruch from the north. Soon we are in touch with the control tower, which advises us about the state of the wind, which has increased since our departure.

We hold formation till the last possible second – a tactic designed to minimize the danger of last-minute attack by enemy aircraft. Then we do a defensive break – a hard turn at three-second intervals that puts the aeroplanes in line astern. As we turn downwind each pilot takes up separation from the aircraft ahead until we are all a thousand yards apart.

Air-traffic control gives us permission to land. 'Three greens,' the Boss announces, confirming he has the three green lights on his instrument panel which show that the landing gear is locked down. With no fuss or hesitation we go straight in. The Boss puts us down hard and clean on the near end of the runway, with hundreds of yards of spare concrete ahead of us. Almost at once he eases across to the left-hand side. 'I'm just getting over in case Number Three has to come hurtling by us.' While we are taxiing towards the hardened shelter he opens the canopy and blessedly cool fresh air floods in. The relief is wonderful. Although I had not actually been sick, I had felt peculiar, to say the least, since the beginning of the dogfight.

Back on the Squadron, Flt Lt Trinder goes through every facet of the sortie in the debrief. The aircrew's faces are marked with reddish lines where their oxygen masks had pressed into them, but all are lit up by the exhilaration of the trip. The mission as a whole is judged a success, but every attack is carefully analysed, particularly the FRAs on the range. Although the leader's own bomb-runs were excellent, some of the others turned out less than perfect. The errors are criticized quite toughly, but in a constructive way. The SAPs are also run through in detail. If the crews really did make all the hits they claim, the targets would have been totally destroyed – and it is not likely that anybody is exaggerating, for the films, already being developed, will soon expose any excessive optimism.

The hassle with the bogie is dissected with the greatest enthusiasm. What happened, apparently, was that the navigator in Number Three spotted a single Phantom on CAP (combat air patrol) circling leisurely at 3000 feet, in his four o'clock. Seeing the bogie start a dive attack, he called the buster. The formation accelerated, fanning out to present more scattered targets, and in the ensuing mêlée the bogie made several ill-judged moves which would, we reckon, have led to his downfall.

One came as he climbed across the nose of the Boss and myself to make a pass at Number One – hence the agitated cry of 'Camera!' For a few moments the Phantom was right there ahead of us, in easy theoretical range of our Sidewinder missile. Now I cursed myself for having failed even to see him. The second chance came when, having turned away once, the fighter ran in again behind Number Three. That was the moment at which the Boss called for retard defence. In this tactic a Buccaneer releases a 1000-lb bomb, which falls to the ground fractionally retarded by its own parachute and goes off in the face of the enemy. No direct hit is necessary. At really low level the debris thrown up by the explosion will knock down a pursuer at any range up to 3000 yards – and even if it fails to knock him down, it will certainly spoil his aim.

35

Altogether, it is decided that the Phantom would certainly have been shot down, but that he might have taken out one of our formation first. The moral is: keep an even better look-out; see him first; sharpen up.

Even the Boss admits the 100-minute sortie was hard work. As for me – I am left so exhausted, physically and mentally, that later in the day I cannot even remember my own telephone number when I try to give it to a friend. For me the flight was a shattering and memorable experience; but for the crews of 16 Squadron it was merely one more routine training sortie in their endless preparation for a war which they hope will never come.

The Beginning

On Sunday, 21 May 1978, thirty-four young men hoping to become officers in the Royal Air Force were expected at the Officers and Aircrew Selection Centre at Biggin Hill, just outside Bromley, on the southern fringes of London. Attracted by advertisements in the national press, by recruiting shows and films and posters, or just by the remarks of friends and family, they had all taken the trouble to go to a local recruiting office and fill in the appropriate form. Even so, as usual a few lost their nerve at the last minute and did not turn up, so that only thirty-one checked in. Of these, one withdrew when he saw more clearly what was going to be involved, leaving thirty candidates to go through the selection process.

Those who came by car drove into trouble some time before they reached their destination, for although it was late in the afternoon the annual Biggin Hill air show was still in progress, and enormous traffic jams choked the roads all round the airfield. So hard was it to make progress that several of the candidates abandoned their cars and walked the last two or three miles to make sure they were not late.

The size and popularity of the air show gave the more thoughtful of them an inkling of the fact that Biggin Hill had once been a famous RAF station. Now the airfield is in civilian hands and the RAF merely uses some of the buildings for administrative purposes; but the Spitfire and Hurricane that stand guard on either side of the entrance to the Selection Centre confirm that the airfield's fame dates from the second world war. During the Blitz Biggin Hill lay directly under the flightpath of the German bombers approaching London, and during the five years of the war the fighter squadrons based here shot down no fewer than 1400 enemy aircraft. Yet the young men reporting for selection were not thinking of the past. Their minds were focused firmly forwards on the possibility of becoming RAF pilots. It was probably fortunate that they did not know the relevant statistics, for these suggested that no more than two of the thirty would pass out to fly fast jets.

Their backgrounds differed widely. One or two were married, most single. Several were already serving in the RAF as airmen, a few had civilian jobs, but most came straight from school or university. Almost all looked neat and clean in suits or sports jackets: flared trousers and high Cuban heels were much in evidence, and although hair tended to be long, it was well styled and cut.

Soon after they had assembled, they were given a short introductory talk by the Station Duty Officer, Squadron Leader Dodds, who welcomed them to Biggin Hill and explained the procedures they would be going through. The talk took place in the reception room, which was to be the focal point of the candidates' existence during the next two days. It was there that they passed the time between the various tests, and there that they waited anxiously to hear the news, good or bad. The receptionist, Julie, became a key figure in their brief but traumatic stay: it was she who directed them from one test to the next and kept check of their progress.

Squadron Leader Dodds had a nice line in heavy settling jokes. The aptitude and medical tests would take place at the same time as the interviews, he explained, so that it was possible someone might be called away for interview in the middle of his medical. 'Don't worry,' he said cheerfully. 'We'll give you time to put your trousers back on!' He apologized for the fact that nerve-racking delays would be inevitable, and pointed out that the reception area had a good stock of magazines, as well as a video system on which candidates could watch various RAF publicity films.

An informal discussion held after supper in the Candidates' Club – a sort of junior officers' mess – revealed a variety of reasons for wanting to join up. Paradoxical as it may sound (for flying military jets can hardly be considered the safest of occupations), the reason most often given was that the RAF offers *security*: a good and interesting job, and long-term career prospects. Several of the candidates were already disillusioned with their civilian jobs, which they found too boring, and wanted something with more challenge and excitement. Others were discouraged by the difficulty of finding jobs at all. Some of the young men merely wanted to fly, others to join because their fathers had been in the RAF, or because they had some other family connection with the Service. On the whole, however, motives were practical rather than idealistic. Patriotism may have played some part, but in the bar no one was going to admit that he wanted to defend Queen and country against their enemies.

Next morning reveille was at 6.30, breakfast at 6.45, and the first call to Part One of the selection process at 7.30. Some candidates went first for their medicals and some for aptitude testing. This last was the most amusing for the participants. Part mechanical and part intellectual, the aptitude tests are designed to discover whether or not a person has the basic physical co-ordination and intelligence to fly aeroplanes. Like the medicals, they are exclusive: that is to say, anybody failing to reach a certain standard is automatically disqualified from pilot training.

The first – known as a Controlled Velocity Test – gauges the smoothness of co-ordination between hand and eye. Each candidate sits confronted by a drum, vertically mounted, which revolves when he switches it on. A pointer, poised over the surface of the drum, can be moved to left and right by means of a steering wheel on the front of each desk. The aim is to make the tip of the pointer pass over as many as possible of the dots that snake in irregular lines round the revolving surface. It is a bit like driving a racing car on a slot-machine at a fair-ground, but more difficult, since the movement of the pointer lags behind that of the steering wheel. Cheating is impossible, for the score from each machine is recorded automatically.

The sergeant in charge took great trouble to make sure everybody understood what had to be done. He explained the procedure twice, then gave the word of command for a practice run. 'Ready?' he asked. 'Hands on switches. Switches on!'

The candidates concentrated furiously, hunched over their drums with furrowed brows. Their nervousness showed in speeded-up breathing and in the frantic snatching movements with which they jerked their wheels back and forth. The scores of their three runs were recorded, but not passed on to them.

The next test, known as Sensory Motor Application, judged the ability to co-ordinate hand, foot and eye movements. Here each person sits before a small television screen with a bright spot of light at its centre. A control column, like one in an aircraft, governs up-and-down movement of the spot, a rudder bar operated by the feet the lateral movement. When the operator switches on, the spot begins to veer outwards randomly from the middle, and the candidate's task is to keep it as near the centre of the screen as he can. Every time it goes outside the small rectangle marked on the screen, the apparatus gives a click, and he incurs penalty points.

Again the sergeant made it all as simple as possible: 'On this machine, you'll be given three short tests . . . and I shall not be able to give you any further instructions once the test has begun. Before the start of each machine run, I shall use the following and cautionary words: "Ready . . . spot central . . . controls steady . . . carry on." '

Once more the concentration was intense. The test – apparently straightforward – generated an amazing amount of psychological pressure. People steered frantically and kicked desperately at the rudder bars, their anxiety heightened by the clicking of the machine whenever their spot veered out of the control panel.

The pressure was still worse in the written tests, which are all races against the clock: fifteen questions have to be answered in twelve minutes, sixty in fifty minutes, and so on. Almost all the problems have a strong visual element: from a row of five geometrical patterns, for example, the candidate has to select the odd one out. The first questions are very simple, like those in a child's puzzle book, but they gradually become more difficult and more concerned with flying: in some the candidate has to interpret representations of flying instruments and say which way the aircraft would be heading or turning.

In fact each person is getting a small foretaste of what will confront him during pilot training and later, when he is on his own in the air. Then, as now, problems will come at him faster than he can deal with them; he will have to make instant decisions, to put each decision straight behind him and look ahead to the next, above all to keep cool.

For their medicals, by contrast, the candidates could do nothing to help themselves. They were literally in the hands of the doctors, for as long as three hours, so stringent are the checks made. Perfect eyesight is obviously one indispensable requirement, and it is a great shock for some people to discover that they are colour blind. Having never realized there was anything wrong, they are dismayed to find that they cannot pick out the patterns and numbers that others easily detect in the circles full of coloured dots. Another necessity for anyone who hopes to fly high-performance aeroplanes is a straightforward arrangement of breathing

41

tubes, particularly sinuses. People with crooked noses are often rejected first time, but encouraged to have their noses straightened and then apply again – not for cosmetic reasons, but simply because bent nasal passages may cause severe problems if the owner goes through rapid pressure changes.

One part of the medical is physical measurement. Each candidate's vital statistics are recorded with an accuracy denied even to models or film stars. Not only height and girth, but also length of arm, thigh and lower leg, and width of hips, are minutely measured on an ingenious built-in system of hinged and sliding rulers. The point is to make sure that the person will fit into the narrow confines of a fast jet's cockpit, the practical height limit being not much over six feet.

On the whole the candidates were resigned about their medicals. Although in prospect the examination seemed daunting, they knew they could do nothing to influence its outcome, so that if they failed, the fault was in no way theirs. Yet they were uneasily fascinated by the close attention paid to their size. They had already heard horror stories of men losing their knee-caps on the under-side of the instrument panel during ejection from Lightnings, and now the reality of what they were letting themselves in for suddenly seemed much closer.

For most of them, the worst part of the whole procedure was the delay between tests. 'It was terrible sitting waiting for the buzzer to go,' said one of them, Trevor Lewis. 'All the time you were expecting your name to be called out, not knowing whether you'd be going on to the medical or for a quick walk – pack your case and walk out of the gates. When you were actually doing something, it wasn't too bad, but hanging around was a killer.'

Of the actual Part One procedures, the most dreaded was the interview. Although candidates had been assured that they would just have a friendly conversation with the officers who form the interview board, they knew that a lot depended on their giving good accounts of themselves. Their apprehension was not misplaced, for the Part One interview was indeed the most critically revealing stage of their examination. It is during this long talk that the boarding officers really get a smell of whether the candidate is going to suit the RAF or not. The interview may not be scientifically devised or psychologically precise, but it does yield the basic information that the boarding officers need.

The interviews take place in small, bare rooms, with the candidate facing the two boarding officers across a wooden table. The officers sit side by side, with forms and folders spread out on the table, and, wedged into the slightly-open drawers in such a position as to be invisible to the candidate, cards bearing tables of reminders.

Inevitably, a good deal depends on the candidate's appearance and on the initial impact he makes. The officers train themselves to ignore the first impression as much as they can, for they know that, having personal biases of their own, they may be misled by superficial details. All the same, a young man who is clean and tidily dressed has a better chance of impressing them than someone who is scruffy.

In 1978 nobody minded if a candidate had long hair, provided his appearance was not too extreme. 'If someone comes in with hair down to his waist and beads round his neck, it *is* difficult,' one officer conceded. 'You may need five minutes or so to get acclimatized to the person, and then you may start to see there is something under it, after all. But normally long hair doesn't worry us – not at all.'

Another question which used to cause much agonizing was that of accents: forty years ago, they had to be right. Now nobody cares in the least about a man's accent – unless it is so extreme as to be unintelligible over a radio link.

The quality being sought, more than any other, is determination. In any discussion of pilot training, at whatever stage, this is the word that crops up most frequently: what fast-jet pilots need above all else is determination and tenacity. Hence the boarding officers' interest in the candidate's sporting achievements. It is not that they particularly *admire* success in sport: rather, that they see it as a sign of determination and the will to succeed.

All the interviews take much the same shape. For the first half, one officer questions the candidate about his background, parents, home, school career and any other achievements so far. Then the bowling changes ends, so to speak, and the second officer comes on for a few overs about why the applicant wants to become an RAF pilot. This – though it may not appear so to the applicant – is really the key issue, the most important question. If he cannot show real enthusiasm about joining, and back it up with reasonable knowledge about what aircraft the RAF flies, and what its role is within NATO and at home, he is not likely to get a high mark. A disappointingly large proportion of candidates produce only superficial reasons for wanting to become pilots, and make it all too clear that they have not entertained the idea for long.

Some questions are less innocent than they sound. A common one, for instance, asks how far it was from home to school. The officer's aim, of course, is not to find out that simple fact, but to see what clues he can pick up as to the young man's determination. Could he be bothered to make that journey to school again in the evenings, for extra-curricular activities?

Both questioners naturally follow up any lead that looks interesting, but they never press hard. If someone starts to make a fool of himself by talking nonsense, they do not drive him into a corner but ease off and head in some other direction. The result is that almost every candidate finds, to his slight surprise, that he comes out having positively enjoyed his interview – and also having learned something about himself.

Very few of the questions are framed formally, but

one that is concerns criminal records: 'Bearing in mind the Rehabilitation of Offenders Act, we ask you the question: "What trouble, if any, have you had with the police?" ' Other standard inquiries seek to elicit the high spot and low spot of the candidate's life so far. Though most of the answers are humdrum, some are far from routine. One boy, when asked why he did not apply to become a civilian pilot, replied that there would be less chance of being hijacked if he were in the RAF; and another demonstrated his grasp of military aviation by maintaining that a Buccaneer pilot never looks out of his cockpit, but has a periscope with which to see the target.

Some candidates are doomed before they start – though they do not know it – by the reports or letters of headmasters and employers, which the boarding officers have read. One recent applicant came hopefully to interview little realizing that his headmaster had written: 'He showed no determination in school matters, except to do as little as possible.' Another man arrived prematurely damned by his tutor: 'I cannot recommend Mr X as a member of our armed forces . . . in fact I would feel safer if he were on the other side.'

No matter how unpromising, every candidate is given a full forty or forty-five minutes; even if the boarding officers quickly sense that someone is not going to meet their requirements, they still give him the full treatment – partly to ensure that they themselves have not made a premature judgement, and partly to forestall the possibility of a disgruntled candidate going off and complaining that he did not get a proper hearing. One thing which instantly undermines a candidate is any attempt to shoot lines or put something over on the board. The officers have seen it all before, too often, and the only positive advice they can give is to be natural.

The interview is designed to find out as much as possible about a candidate's personality, to test his motivation and to judge his powers of expression. At this stage his character can be judged only from school or other reports, which should mention his good or bad qualities. Part Two of the selection process, however, is principally a test of temperament: it aims to find out how an individual reacts in a group, and how he behaves under pressure.

After the interview the boarding officers allot every candidate a rating, from seven ('Excellent – almost a ready-made officer. Virtually no chance of failure); through six ('Good'); five ('Promising'); four ('Moderate'); three ('Uncertain'); two ('Weak'); to one and nought ('Unsuitable. Has character defects or holds views incompatible with military service'). All those from seven to four inclusive go into training automatically. Those with nought or one fail, and those with two or three *may* go into training, depending on how they do in Part Two of the selection process.

A very large proportion of the candidates fall into the two-three band. When they have left the room, the interviewing officers spend a considerable amount of time discussing their merits and trying to agree on a common mark. Is X a two-plus going towards two-and-a-half, or a three-minus also inclining towards two-and-a-half?

The RAF is sometimes accused by other training organizations of being too harsh in its selection procedures: certainly the rejection rate is high, but experience has repeatedly shown that the RAF cannot afford to lower its standards.

This particular group seemed better than most. Only two people failed their aptitude tests and two their medicals – both figures being lower than normal. Four more were eliminated by the Part One interviews. The man who shouldered the uncomfortable task of telling people they had failed was the Review Officer of the day, Wing Commander Simpson. His manner was admirable – straightforward and brisk, but at the same time sympathetic. 'I'm afraid I've got disappointing news for you,' he began. He was quickest with the men already in the RAF, who called him 'Sir' and were required to sign a form agreeing they understood what they had been told. The civilians signed no form and were given a little more time. Although most took the bad news well, one or two burst into tears. Wing Commander Simpson, being a practical man, kept a box of Scotties in his desk against such emergencies.

Several of those who did not quite make the grade for pilot opted to go for navigator instead and were fed back into the selection process. The rejected airmen returned to their units, and the dud civilians were sent straight off on what is known as the Four-Ten procedure, this being the number of the bus service to Bromley station.

Thus, at one stage or another, nine of the original thirty-one candidates were eliminated, and twenty-two went forward into the more demanding Part Two of the selection. The survivors were split up into groups of five or six, each assigned a letter. Now they all wore grey overalls and blue bibs with bold white letters and numbers on them, front and back – A 1, A 2, and so on. Henceforth they were referred to by numbers rather than by names; the numbers had nothing to do with the grades awarded after interview, but were for ease and speed of identification.

The survivors also had their photographs taken in groups of five or six. The snapshots were constantly referred to by the boarding officers as they made their assessments, particularly when they were writing up their reports, and a persistent rumour had it that one of their wives could unfailingly predict, from a perusal of the rogues' gallery, who would pass and who would fail.

The first exercise of Part Two, known as Leaderless, took place in the gym (in fact a hangar). Each group was confronted with a short obstacle course and a peculiar-looking selection of equipment with which to cross the (imaginary) chasms and minefields between habitable platforms: a plank, a round pole, a short piece of rope, a stout wooden cross and a five gallon oil drum. The group was given one minute in which to make a compulsory survey, and then twenty minutes in which to transport all its members and equipment from the start line to the finish. If anyone touched down in one of the 'black' or out-of-bounds areas, he incurred a penalty, which took the form of being sent back a stage.

The exercise looks like a game, but in fact is carefully devised. Invented by the Germans before the second world war, it was originally used by the Wehrmacht to show up people who become neurotic in unstructured situations. The RAF uses it more as a settling-down exercise, but finds that it can be most revealing.

'On the subject of nerves,' said the officer in charge. 'It would be surprising if you weren't feeling nervous, but you'll be OK as soon as you start. Once the exercise *has* started, we will answer no further questions . . . All the problems can be solved in more ways than one, but *against the clock* . . . Remember, we're looking not just for leaders, but for good team mates as well, so be your natural selves . . .'

The exercise calls for a certain amount of physical strength and agility, but even more for quick thinking and foresight. Somebody, for instance, must appreciate that it is better to reserve the smallest and lightest members of the group for certain roles: although there is some hope that the big fellows will be able to hoist them on the end of a plank, there is no hope that they will be able to hoist the heavies.

Soon every team was in desperate contortions, with the victims of overambitious schemes collapsing into the black areas between safe stations or having to be dragged unceremoniously back from the brink of disaster. The invigilating officers prowled round with stop-watches and clip boards, taking notes on individual reactions and raising the pressure with occasional reminders about how little time was left. 'Did I see a black foot there, Number Two?'

Failure to finish the course did not count greatly against a team or any of its members. More important was the question of whether or not they had worked together well, and whether any individuals had shown particular initiative. Yet there were pitfalls for the over-enthusiastic: a desire to impress the observers with exemplary leadership qualities could easily seduce someone into a rash decision and leave him stuck with a totally unworkable solution.

Next came a discussion period, for which the team sat at tables arranged in a shallow crescent. Although the members did not know it, they were positioned so that the ones who had scored highest in the interviews were on the outside ends of the line: if the two brightest people in the group tried to monopolize the conversation, they had to do so across everybody else, thus giving others a better chance to break in.

The subjects were hoary old chestnuts, such as 'Do newspapers mould or follow public opinion?' 'Has the monarchy still a useful role in this country?' 'Are soft drugs dangerous?' The officer in charge repeated the subject twice and let the group talk about it for four or five minutes. Then he rapped on the table – no matter what stage the discussion had reached – and threw another subject into the ring. All the time he and a colleague were making notes on how each candidate performed – how much he put into the discussion, whether what he said was intelligent or superficial, and how easily he was swayed from his opinion.

After thirty minutes and five or six subjects, the period closed. The candidates regrouped their tables to form an inward-facing L for the next phase – a planning exercise. In this the group, working as a team, had to work out a plan for rescuing a party of explorers trapped in a hostile country. A sketch map and written brief outlined the position and the facilities available: there were basically three different permutations to be worked out for the rescue journey – three possible combinations of voyage by boat and overland

49

trek. The group had half an hour in which to prepare its plan. The officers then questioned individuals on particular aspects of the rescue. Finally, every candidate was required to write an essay describing the plan in full.

Afterwards, many confessed that they found this extremely difficult. The problem was worst for those – the majority – who had had a scientifically based education. Since leaving school, or even since they did English for O-levels, they had got out of the habit of writing continuous prose, and found it hard to express themselves clearly. If they did, it was unfortunate, for, like the aptitude tests, the essay can prove a knockout punch: someone who cannot express himself at all on paper is never going to make an RAF officer, and an unsatisfactory essay can channel a candidate straight into the Four-Ten procedure.

The essay brought the day's tests to an end. In the evening the surviving candidates got a foretaste of life in an RAF officers' mess. At the Candidates' Club, which has a spacious ante-room, a bar and a games room, they were expected to wear jackets and ties. Contrary to general belief, they were not spied on by members of the staff while drinking and relaxing, as happens with candidates in the Navy. The evening really was their own.

The following morning they started off in the hangar with the Individual Plan. Again, the teams were required to cross an obstacle course, but this time one man was in charge of each: it was up to him to devise schemes that would work and drive them through – all against the clock. The fact that one person was suddenly in the spotlight, depended on by the rest of the team and watched by several officers, put enormous pressure on him. In the words of one of the directing staff, 'If you find yourself in the middle of no-man's land, with three guys stuck on the beam, one upside-down, and no one able to go forward or back, you have to pull your finger out.' The stress of this exercise generally produces valuable clues about a person's temperament: the staff now start to get a real glimpse of how he reacts under difficulties.

Back in the interview room, the spotlight was again put on one person at a time with the Individual Problem. Each candidate was confronted with a brief similar to that used for the group planning session the day before, but this time he had to work out a solution, and justify it, on his own.

In one scenario he was the leader of an RAF mountain-rescue team required to rescue two climbers with broken legs from Mulligan Peak. At his disposal were a Land-Rover, a boat with a temporarily broken-down engine, and a stretcher party. Given the lengths of the various routes and the speeds at which the different forms of transport could move, he had to work out the best possible method of getting the injured men to hospital.

Another scenario made him the captain of the Boxton football team due to play a match against Holt, twenty-six miles away. Already it was midday, and the coach supposed to be taking the team had broken down. The only other transport available consisted of one bicycle and an ancient Ford Anglia with its wheels off . . .

Once the leader had made his plan, the boarding officers went through it with him step by step. The merits or demerits of the plan were obviously an important factor; yet it was the vigour and resource with which he justified it that won him most marks in the end. By casting doubts, by challenging his calculations, the boarding officers put him under quite severe pressure – and it was the way in which he reacted that interested them.

After the Individual Problem, all that remained was the final interview. Compared with the all-important Part One interview, this was almost a formality – a summing-up, and an opportunity for the candidate to ask questions. After that he was free to leave – without knowing whether he had passed or not. The Air

Board's final deliberations about each candidate were long and careful, especially in borderline cases. The officers were, after all, deciding whether or not to spend at least £1 million putting an individual through the training programme. Here were two of the boarding officers talking about a promising candidate.

A: 'He's got a good record of academic achievement, as well as sporting activities and other outside interests. They suggest, in fact, a man of some breadth and depth, and a sense of responsibility. His sports include the beefy ones like rugby and football, as well as those requiring good co-ordination of hand and eye, like tennis and squash . . . On these grounds, at least, he ought not to have too much trouble with the elementary handling.

'But he's got to be able to think quickly in the air, and here really comes the first of two reservations I have about him. He's got a remarkable ability to probe and present detail, but because of this he tended to choose unnecessarily complex solutions – sometimes a bit unrealistic. In other respects, however, his mind was quick and flexible and quite effective, and I think that in officer training the influence of his mates around him, and certainly the influence of his flight commander, together with the variety of practical problems he'll be set, will help him to bring his intelligence to bear a bit more directly than here. So I don't think this first reservation is too much trouble.

'But the second, which you probably saw as well, concerns his motivation. This seems uncertain, and I don't know how you felt about that.'

'B: 'Well, I think this was my *main* query: there has to be a reservation about his motivation, and also about whether he is likely to stick the service training . . . He's had a range of rather mediocre jobs, and now he's unemployed. He's 22½, and the question is, did you see enough during the boarding procedures to convince you that he will stand up to the training pressures?'

The completed dossiers reached the President of the Board two days after the candidates had left. He confirmed or modified the ratings given, and referred any marginal cases to the Commandant of the Selection Centre, who himself had sat in on as many boards as he could manage. Thus, the Air Selection Board convened a week later and took the final decisions with the greatest possible care.

Altogether, the intake turned out to have been a profitable one for the RAF, which was able to make firm offers to thirteen of the thirty-one candidates. One man was recommended for training as an air electronics operator, two for airman aircrew service as air engineers, three for commissioned service as navigators, and six for commissioned service as pilots.

In all these six the President of the Board saw 'considerable signs of strength'. He found that they possessed not only the basic aptitude for learning to fly, but also the 'stickability', or determination, and depth of character to see them through the tough three-year training. They were therefore all 'sound prospects'. Even so, experience showed that it would be unusual if more than two of them finally passed out to fly fast jets. In the first phase of training – the OCTU – the wastage rate is between fifteen and twenty-five per cent. Basic Flying Training again weeds out about a quarter. Advanced Flying Training and Weapon Training take a smaller toll, but the final stage, the Operational Conversion Unit, generally defeats some ten per cent of the survivors.

Nobody at Biggin Hill is so arrogant as to suppose that the selection system is perfect. The boarding officers recognize that they handle and observe the candidates over a very short period, and that the young men are bound to change as they mature in the next three years. All the same, the RAF knows what it is looking for, and it remains confident that the Biggin Hill procedures form as efficient a first filter as it is able to devise.

3

Six Characters in Search of a Commission

The BBC's original intention was to film all the six candidates selected from the same intake for pilot training; but one of them, Neil Tonkin, decided almost at once to switch over and join the Navy instead of the Air Force. To make up the number, and to retain the correct proportion of choices to rejects, one more recruit, John McCrea, was chosen from another selection batch and added to the team. Thus the six characters in search of a commission, in alphabetical order, were these:

TREVOR LEWIS

Appearance	Tall, dark, slim, round-headed
Age	19.11
Born	Hemel Hempstead, 15 June 1958
Parents	Father: engineering manager, Rolls Royce Small Engine Division
	Mother: part-time assistant in insurance office
Home	Hemel Hempstead
Education	Cavendish Grammar School, Hemel Hempstead
	2 CSE passes
	5 O-levels
	ONC in Electrical and Electronic Engineering

Sports	Outstanding athlete. Speciality – the tetrathlon (300-metre swimming, 4000-metre cross-country running, épée fencing and .22 pistol snap shooting); hockey, squash, weight training, cycling
Hobbies	Go-kart racing and maintenance, chess, reading and writing poetry, walking
Career	Joined RAF as apprentice at RAF Cosford, 1974. Gained ONC, 1977. Posted to RAF Odiham as Junior Technician specializing in air communications and air radar

Marital status Single

A most unusual airman, Trevor Lewis began studying the theory of relativity at the age of thirteen. He plays the trumpet, enjoys the poetry of William Blake, and writes poems himself. Also, he has double-jointed knees which, with a little assistance from someone else, he can turn round so far that his feet face the opposite way to his body. Hence his nickname 'Legs'.

He grew up in a working-class background on a council estate. His boyhood was much influenced by the fact that his father mended mowing machines as a hobby, and it was taken for granted that young Trevor would help with this lucrative side-line, rather than go off and play with friends. The result was that by the age of eleven he could strip, service and reassemble any motor mower in the country, and at twelve he was a proficient car mechanic.

Everyone in his family urged him to become an engineer, but, being determined to fly, and having admired RAF pilots since boyhood, he joined the RAF as an apprentice (itself quite a feat, since the ratio of candidates to places was nearly a hundred to one). His mechanical skill soon led him to the go-kart club at RAF Cosford, and within a few months he was helping to run it, tuning and repairing the machines and coaching other drivers – an experience which (he later reckoned) greatly increased his capacity for leadership. In the strongly physical atmosphere of the station at Cosford, he went in for a lot of sport, including squash, hockey and volley-ball, besides the tetrathlon.

Curiously enough, in somebody so naturally athletic, his one real weakness was his poor co-ordination – something first revealed to him when he went to Biggin Hill in 1975 for a test-in-advance (a special procedure for those between 15½ and 16½ who are keen to become pilots). On that first visit he was told to work hard at his airman training and then apply again.

He obeyed the instructions on all counts, gaining his Ordinary National Certificate with distinctions and being posted to Odiham, where he worked for nearly a year on Puma and Wessex helicopters. He also made strenuous efforts to improve his co-ordination by means of games like squash and tennis. A quick trip to Germany and an attachment to Northern Ireland gave him a glimpse of life at the sharp end of the Air Force and, if anything, increased his determination to become a pilot.

On his second visit to Biggin Hill, the Board had no doubt about his motivation: he had already shown that he was determined on an air-force career. To one of the boarding officers he seemed a 'dynamic, bright young chap, with a number of really first-class qualities about him, precisely the kind of chap we're looking for'. There could be no question of his determination to stick with it during training if things got difficult for him.

The one serious reservation about him was again his co-ordination. Although it had improved since his first visit to the OASC, it was still poor, and his score in the aptitude tests was marginal – the lowest with which he could have passed. This, the Board admitted, meant there was an element of risk in their recommending him for pilot training; but they believed that his other good qualities would get him through.

Another handicap was the phenomenal speed at which he talked. Often he spoke in such a rush as to be hard to follow: at a briefing, or, worse still, over a radio link, he might well be incomprehensible. But this was something that could obviously be worked on. His quick mind, ebullient sense of humour and boundless optimism, together with his exceptional physical fitness, made him an immediately attractive candidate for training.

ROBBIE LOW

Appearance	Tall, slim, dark, slitty-eyed, straight hair cut in fringe. Pronounced Scottish accent
Age	21
Born	Perth, 21 April 1957
Parents	Father: Foreman Maintenance Engineer with Dewar's Distillery, Perth
	Mother: Sales and general assistant, Caithness Glass
Home	Perth
Education	Perth Academy
	9 Ordinary grades
	5 Highers
Sports	Hockey, squash, badminton
Hobbies	Boys Brigade
Career	Training as state-registered nurse at the Perth College of Nursing
Marital status	Single

When Low's dossier came before the final Board, it occupied them for a shorter time than anyone else's. They saw him as 'a very sound young man all round' with 'a great respect for the Service'. To one officer he was 'quite a plucky young lad, with a lot of determination and stamina when the going got tough – a

Scotty, in fact'. Nobody had any reservations at all, and he was passed straight away.

On paper, this looked a strange result, for the idea of becoming a killer pilot would appear to have been totally at variance with the career on which he had already launched himself – that of a state-registered nurse. Realizing that at his interview one of the key questions would be about how he explained the sudden switch, he arrived with a well thought-out answer. As a nurse, he told the boarding officers, he did what was best for his patients; but if, as an RAF officer, he found himself obliged to kill some of the country's enemies, that, too, would be the best he could do for his compatriots. The Board seemed impressed with this argument.

By the time he was seventeen Low decided that he had had enough of sitting in a classroom. He therefore did not apply for a place at university, but enlisted for a three-year course at the Perth College of Nursing. Two factors in particular drew him to train as a nurse: first, the knowledge that he would be working with people; and second, the fact that he would be actually doing the job while he learned. He learned a great deal, not least in the various hospital departments, including casualty, to which he was attached. But after eighteen months or so he came to see that, if he was eventually promoted, he would be unable to do any more nursing (which he enjoyed) as he would automatically become an administrator.

Already, as a boy, he had thought of joining the armed forces, and now, while he was having doubts, his eye fell on one of the RAF's newspaper advertisements for pilots. Following it up at the Careers Office in Dundee, he was shown RAF films, which increased his enthusiasm for the idea of learning to fly, and in due course the Office arranged his visit to Biggin Hill.

His marked Scots accent slightly worried one of the boarding officers; but, as with Trevor Lewis, it was agreed that, if necessary, he could be taught to speak more slowly.

Appearance	Stocky, sandy receding fair hair
Age	22.11
Born	Stockport, 5 June 1955
Parents	Father: civil servant
	Mother: civil servant
Home	Marple, Stockport
Education	Marple Hall Grammar School
	11 O-levels
	3 A-levels
	Newcastle University, left after one year
Sports	Rugby, Volleyball
Hobbies	Fast cars, car maintenance, trials motorbikes, sound recording
Career	Coalman
	Farm labourer
	Milkman
Marital status	Single

From his record John McCrea did not look a likely starter in the pilot stakes. His career so far has been unsatisfactory, a series of starts, stops and failures to achieve full potential.

He is of medium height and stocky build, with reddish fair hair already receding from his forehead and a wispy reddish moustache. His Cheshire origin shows in his pleasant northern accent. It is a clear indication of the pecking-order at home that, although he knows his mother works as a civil servant at the job centre in Marple, he is not sure exactly what his father does: he too is a civil servant, and John *thinks* he works in the Department of Health and Social Security, but he is not certain.

At Marple Hall Grammar School John did exceptionally well in his O-levels, finishing with eleven passes, taken in three separate batches. But his A-levels proved disappointing: a B in General Studies, a D in Physics, an E in Mathematics, and a failure in Chemistry. He was hardly surprised by the low grades, because he already knew himself well enough to recognize that he was lazy. He did not work hard, and lacked motivation. Besides, he had a girl friend and a motor bike, and they both took up time.

Nor was he helped by the advice of the Careers Officer at school. Because, since the age of twelve, John had done part-time work on a nearby farm, the officer brushed aside his statement that he would like to be a pilot and directed him instead towards agriculture. He therefore opted to read agricultural engineering when he went to Newcastle University.

Again he made little effort. He found it impossible to get down to work, and somehow never fitted into life at university. One reason was that he went home every weekend, to see family and friends, and never became much involved in university affairs. Looking back later, he felt sure he could have passed the exams if he had stuck the course. But at the time the prospect of yet more exams seemed infinitely depressing: he had sat exam papers of one kind or another every summer for the past four years. So, having failed the first-year papers twice, he decided to take a year off. His aim was to return eventually and complete the course, but in the end he never did.

With his mother in the job centre, it was easy for him to find work. He became a coalman in Marple, driving a lorry and delivering coal all round his home area. Being a physical, outdoor type, he enjoyed the job, which was strenuous; he also liked earning the good money it paid – he was taking home £45 a week, and that in 1975 – for he hated having to ask his parents for cash, and his work gave him a kind of independence.

In the spring a full-time job became available on the farm belonging to Conrad and Gordon Clark, where he had worked intermittently since he was a boy, and he took it gladly, farm work being what he liked best. At first he was a general labourer, but soon the girl who did the milk round left, so he took over her job as well. This meant getting up at 5 a.m., loading the van, and setting off on the delivery round with a lad as a helper. Back at the farm by 10 o'clock, he would turn to general work, not finishing until 4 p.m. Again, he earned good money; but after a period of satisfaction he began to find the work monotonous. Because so little thought was needed, he could feel his brain shutting down. He saw that he was turning into a vegetable, becoming, in his own words, 'even more boring than normal'. What made everything worse was that he saw few friends, being too exhausted after his early starts to go out in the evenings. Gradually he realized that, although he did not mind being a 22-year-old milkman, he did not relish the prospect of being a 40-year-old one.

At the same time his love of flying began to assert itself and his thoughts turned to the idea of a career as a pilot, either in British Airways or in the RAF. One day he chanced to see, lying on the office desk, a letter from a flying club in Manchester, offering a trial lesson for only £10. He did not know if either of the Clark brothers was planning to take lessons or not, but he himself immediately followed up the offer. Having known the farmers for years, and not wanting to seem disloyal, he slid off for the the first lesson in secret. At once he was hooked. Flying became a passion, and whenever he could afford it he bought another lesson, slipping away on Tuesday afternoons, which he had free. Before long he had accumulated ten flying hours.

He then applied to British Airways for a job, but was never even summoned for interview. Disgusted by this slovenly attitude, he tried the RAF – and was promptly invited to go for selection at Biggin Hill. Wanting to keep open as many options as possible, and warned by his chronic lack of self-confidence that he would probably not get through the selection process, he still did not tell the Clarks what he was doing, and took a week's holiday. Then, to his considerable surprise, he found the RAF had accepted him for training.

By then he was walking a financial tightrope. Always a devil for fast transport, he had recently bought a Spitfire sports car with the help of a £1500 bank loan. On the farm he was earning enough to pay off the instalments of the loan, but he knew that his initial pay in the RAF would be much less. He could hardly afford to join up with the loan still running; yet he could not afford to defer his application, for he was already approaching the upper age limit accepted by the Air Force for civilian entrants. He therefore had only a narrow gap at which to aim.

In any case, he got through it. At Biggin Hill his university failure and the low level of his subsequent jobs both told against him, but in the view of the boarding officers these defects were outweighed by his manifest enthusiasm for flying and his determination to take to the air.

MARTIN OXBORROW

Appearance	Big, strong, reddish-fair hair
Age	25.11
Born	Ipswich, 30 May 1952
Parents	Father: manager for Fisons Fertilisers
	Mother: part-time assistant in Boots
Home	Felixstowe
Education	Felixstowe Grammar School
	5 O-levels
	5 City & Guild qualifications in motor technology at Ipswich Civic College
Sports	Soccer, badminton, sailing
Hobbies	Guitar-playing, car-maintenance, cooking

Career	Four-year apprenticeship with Mann Egerton, Ipswich
	One year as skilled mechanic
	Three years as car salesman
	Joined RAF as airman, 31 March 1976
	Present occupation: Weapons technician at RAF Marham
Marital status	Married for just over a year. Wife Anne-Marie works as hotel receptionist in King's Lynn

Oxborrow was already on the upper age limit for pilot training, and the boarding officers seemed a little puzzled by the twists and turns of his career. His record at Felixstowe Grammar School was sound, if undistinguished. Having tried for eight O-levels, he passed five, and then, when he was sixteen, he decided to leave school rather than go for A-levels. His decision was much influenced by the example of his elder brother, who had been forced to remain at school by his parents longer than he wanted, had failed to pass the A-levels, which were the reason for his staying on, and had then found himself in a rut.

Rather than get trapped in a similar position, Martin took up an apprenticeship with Mann Egerton, the motor distributors. After four years he completed the apprenticeship successfully and spent another twelve months working for the firm as a skilled mechanic. Then he trained as a car salesman, still aiming to make his career in the motor industry, but in 1974 decided to follow his brother's example and join the RAF. Rejected for pilot-training, he went back to selling cars. Finally, in March 1976, he did join the Air Force as an aircraftman.

The Board was impressed by the range of his outside interests. He had owned a guitar since the age of eleven and had played in several groups. He had travelled a good deal in Europe. He had shown a genuine interest in flying by taking lessons (which he paid for himself until they became too expensive) and by gliding. He played a lot of badminton.

When asked why he wanted to become an officer, he replied that his experience of RAF life so far had made him feel he could go further. As part of the ground crew, he said, he saw the aircraft go off, and did the work on them when they came back. 'But the guy in the cockpit is doing the top job in the Air Force. He's in charge of a very expensive piece of machinery, and absolutely in the front line.'

When asked what he felt about the idea of being used as cannon fodder, should war break out in Europe, he replied that he had thought hard about the possibility. 'If I was a young man with a family, working as a civilian in England, I reckon I would expect somebody to be defending the country anyway. I certainly think I could do it – and I want to do it.'

As the high spot in his life so far he gave the moment when he passed out to become a skilled mechanic; and as the low spot, the car crash in 1968 which left him with multiple injuries and put him out of work for six months.

Altogether, he made a good impression on the Board, but he also left the officers with certain doubts. They found him smart, lively and intelligent, but wondered whether he had the necessary staying power. The fluctuations of his career to date worried them, as did his age. They were not sure how he would perform in a group. But they decided that he had potential for commissioned service and put him through.

The fact that he was already married worried one member of the final Board. At OCTU no wives are allowed, and all cadets have to live in. This meant that Mrs Oxborrow would have to be parked somewhere else. How would they both manage? Because they had no children yet, the Board decided that things should not be too difficult for them. Nevertheless, the reservation was a prophetic one.

Appearance	Slim, fair-haired, youthful
Age	20.7
Born	Acton, 24 August 1957
Parents	Father: retired, formerly publican
	Mother: formerly a nurse
Home	Bedfordshire
Education	Dunstable Grammar School
	8 O-levels
	ONC Mechanical Engineering
Sports	Rugby, hockey, water polo
Hobbies	Clay-pigeon shooting
Career	Joined RAF as apprentice airman, 1974
	Present occupation: Air Fitter on
	Lightnings at RAF Binbrook
Marital status	Single, but steady girl friend

With his grey, three-piece suit and boldly-striped shirt, Smart was one of the dressiest candidates at the Selection Centre. His soft fair hair and peaches-and-cream complexion made him look young and vulnerable, and indeed it was the verdict of one of his boarding officers that although he had 'quite a nice façade, quite a nice shell, once you get inside that shell there's not very much to offer'.

During his interview he made one serious mistake in a subject on which – having already served four years in the RAF – he should have been particularly strong. Questioned about the roles of various different aircraft, he was asked the probable price of a Tornado. He gave it as £1½ million, when the proper answer was £9 million. To the Board this seemed symptomatic of his generally shallow grasp of current affairs. Thus, after the Part One interview, his chances of being selected seemed poor.

In Part Two of the selection process, however, he improved. In both the leadership exercise and the

Individual Plan he impressed the staff by sticking to the solutions he proposed: he remained calm under pressure, took decisions, and stood by them, even if they were not necessarily the right ones. Nor could he be talked out of his choice of action, even by a very persuasive officer.

On the road, his record had been a bit chequered. He had twice been fined for speeding on his motorbike, and was now carless, having had a major accident during the winter. An oncoming driver forced him off the road, and he ended up with his car embedded in a tree, a write-off. The other driver did not even stop, whereas he himself ended up in hospital having his right shoulder x-rayed. That night, he said, was definitely the low point of his life to date.

Other factors, however, were in his favour, among them the good reports from his own RAF station – and his youth: he was thought still young enough to be 'totally receptive to the demands of training'. At the Board which made the final decisions on the candidates, one of the members pointed out that it was more of an ordeal for a serving airman to sit before a panel of senior serving officers than it was for a civilian: maybe this was why Smart had made such a dim showing at his Part One interview.

The Board's decision was that he was of modest but adequate pilot aptitude, and a likely enough prospect to be worth backing.

ALISTAIR STEWART

Appearance	Tall, dark, good-looking
Age	22.6
Born	Hastings, 18 November 1955
Parents	Father: in Colonial Service
	Mother: part-time work in hospital administration
Home	Bexhill

Education	Bexhill Grammar School
	10 O-levels
	3 A-levels
	Newcastle University
	Degree in Zoology
Sports	Golf, squash, tennis, rugby, soccer
Hobbies	Photography, cars, cooking
Career	Worked nine months with wine
	merchants in Newcastle

Marital status Single

Stewart was one of the few candidates ready to admit that he was attracted by the glamour of flying. To be a pilot, he thought, 'is the culmination of everything the Air Force has to offer. It's glamorous, because speed is glamorous, and you think of fast-jet pilots as young blokes with life and energy and go.'

He himself seemed to have plenty of all these assets; but so far he had had a frustrating time in his search for work. Naturally he hoped that his degree in zoology at Newcastle University would qualify him for an interesting job, preferably with an ecological basis, but he was disillusioned by the strength of the competition. He heard that one job, advertised by the Royal Society for the Protection of Birds, with a salary of £3,000, attracted some 1200 applicants.

Stewart impressed his interview board in many ways. They found him articulate, intelligent, mature and relaxed, with considerable strength of personality and depth of character. The one fact about him that worried them was that he seemed to have applied to the RAF only as a last resort, having failed to find a satisfactory civilian job. In other words, his motivation was suspect. Why, if he wanted to fly so badly, had he not shown positive interest in the RAF earlier?

His answers to that question were not particularly convincing. He had thought of doing a Ph.D, but then realized that his academic prowess was not good enough for research work. Flying apart, one thing about the RAF that he said appealed to him was the unity of service life. In a civilian job, he explained, 'you'd go to your office or warehouse or whatever at nine o'clock, you'd finish work at five o'clock, then you'd go home, and that would be it – full stop. In your time off you'd be somebody completely different. So in a sense you'd be leading a bit of a schizophrenic existence . . . I thought it would be better to be in a position where you weren't so much in a job as in a way of life – where your job would *become* your life.'

Another prospect which he said he relished was that of joining a highly skilled team and yet at the same time retaining his individuality. 'Obviously, if you make pilot, you're a member of the team, but you're still an individual – the person who makes some of the decisions.' If he failed for pilot, he said, he would like to be considered for navigator.

In the end the Board decided that, because Stewart had the sort of qualities they were looking for, they could overlook his weak motivation and pass him as 'a justifiable training risk'. As one of the officers put it, 'It's up to us to motivate him.' In effect, they took him on because they liked the look of him, and thought him honest and realistic.

4

The Officer Cadet
Training Unit, Henlow

Alone of all the establishments through which aspiring pilots pass, the Henlow OCTU can be written about in the past tense, for its training function has since been moved to Cranwell, and officer cadets no longer go there.

With only a grass strip, Henlow has never seen heavy flying. All the same, it had a curious history during the second world war, when Italian prisoners of war built the hangars which stand to this day, carving their wooden beams by hand. They also assembled aircraft, which arrived in parts on the railway along one side of the hangars, were put together under cover, and flown out off the grass strip the other side.

Course 329 assembled at Henlow on 3 September 1978, a lovely warm Indian-summer afternoon. Smoke drifted over many of the Bedfordshire fields as farmers burnt off their straw, and in others combine harvesters were still working. Some of the cadets – the less affluent ones, or those whose homes were a great distance away – came out from London by train and were met at Hitchin station by a coach which ran a shuttle service between there and the camp; but all who could arrived in style, driving up in their sports cars to report to the guardroom. None cut a sharper dash than John McCrea in his yellow Morgan coupé, which he himself had rebuilt over the past two years. For an observer posted at the guardroom it was an instructive and amusing spectacle: the young men spruced up to the nines and yet, at the same time, extremely apprehensive as they tried to size up their new surroundings and the calibre of their comrades-to-be.

They were, as they all admitted, thoroughly nervous, particularly the airmen already serving in the RAF, for they had been regaled with horror stories about how tough the regime at Henlow was going to be. What they feared most was the mental rather than the physical stress: it was not the idea of drill and PT and cross-country marches that scared them, but the thought that they might fail.

The normal rules for joining had been bent for the convenience of the BBC film team. Normally the direct-entry cadets who had come straight from civilian life went to OCTU alone, on what was known as the OPC, or Officers' Preparatory Course. The 'hairies' – already veterans of RAF service – usually joined three weeks later on the OMC, or Officers' Main Course. Lewis, Oxborrow and Smart, strictly speaking, belonged to the second category; but to keep the group together as much as possible, they were sent in with the others at the start. The only one of the six not present was Robbie Low, who still had a month of his nurse's training to complete, and so joined the next course, No 330. 'At least if I fail in the RAF I'll have something to fall back on,' he said – a sound, Scottish approach.

Oxborrow, McCrea and Smart were posted to A Flight, under the command of Flt Lt Ollie Delaney. Lewis and Stewart found themselves on B Flight, commanded by Flt Lt Cynthia Fowler. Each flight comprised eight or ten cadets, three of them girls, and since both were part of Red Squadron, all members wore red scarves of identification.

For the first two days their feet, in the old Service phrase, 'hardly touched'. From form-filling to lectures to kit issue to tailor to lectures to barber and back, they hurtled round the camp in a pattern apparently designed to make them travel as far and as fast as possible between appointments. In the middle of the frantic activity they all had to sit down and write a brief essay entitled 'My Life' which summed up their existence to date. They were also issued with loose-leaf diaries, which they were required to bring up to date at the end of every fortnight. To Al Stewart the first two days were 'somewhat daunting', but to John McCrea the rush seemed stimulating, and he found himself thinking clearly 'for the first time in two or three years'.

One task which caused considerable anxiety was the giving of a ten-minute talk to other members of the flight on the same lines as the written essay. Oxborrow in particular found it very alarming, although once he had got over 'the initial horror' of being stared at by people he scarcely knew, he amazed himself by keeping going for eleven minutes.

The first of the numerous lectures came from Group Captain Hutchins, the Station Commander, on the Monday morning. Some people came to Henlow, he warned the cadets, 'with the misguided idea that success on the course is automatic. This is not so. The Queen's commission is earned, and it's not granted lightly. The course is demanding and the standards high.'

In the first four weeks, he said, the newcomers would get an introduction to 'our way of doing things, our language, both spoken and written, and some of our customs. They aren't too strange, but like most large organizations we have our own way of doing things.

'Now, our aim is to pass you all. You're not competing with one another. You're competing with yourself . . . When we put you under pressure, we put you under pressure for a very good reason. We want to find out what your limitations are.

'One thing I will mention here and now . . . you are going to join a *fighting service*. Don't forget that. The

71

emphasis is on fighting and serving. I mention those two words because, as you are only too well aware, we all live in a very imperfect world. Each of you may one day have to fight – either that, or support fighting. So be prepared for it, if it should ever regrettably come about.

'Secondly, there is the word "service". And this is *public* service. At your new level this will carry both privilege and responsibility . . .'

Next in to bat came Chief Instructor, Wing Commander Planterose, who used slides to explain the various stages of the eighteen-week course and also the layout of the camp, which the OCTU shared with a radio engineering unit. Very little flying still took place from the grass airfield, he explained, although a gliding school did use the field at the weekends and on Wednesday afternoons. The bits 'that interest us' were the running track and the two hangars containing an indoor drill hall, a gymnasium and a heated 25-metre swimming pool. Much of his talk emphasized the need for physical fitness.

He also pointed out, on the slides, various prize features of the camp, not least the barber's shop, which the cadets would all be visiting shortly. The grass airfield would become a battleground on which the new recruits would struggle through their early leadership exercises, similar to, but more difficult than, the ones they had done at Biggin Hill. Like the Station Commander, the Chief Instructor ended on a cautionary note: 'We will move heaven and earth to get you up to scratch, but it's no good our dodging the issue and graduating sub-standard officers into an already overstretched Air Force. The overstretch means in effect that when you leave here you will certainly have to be able to pull your own weight in whatever capacity you graduate.'

Whether or not the cadets noticed it, they were fed a few lumps of propaganda in among the practical details of everyday life. Red Squadron's Commanding

Officer, Squadron Leader Bob Slater, gave a brisk pep-talk about such things as the need for punctuality, team-spirit and co-operation, and into the middle of it he slipped some winged words about loyalty and discipline. The RAF, he said, defined loyalty as 'a two-way process', which extended up to the Queen, country, the Service and the Squadron, and down to contemporaries and subordinates. Discipline, he told his new recruits, was the 'very cement of the Service' and the factor that made 'the vital difference' between the civilian and the servicemen. 'Discipline has to be imposed,' he said. 'It doesn't just happen.'

This led him to a rousing action-call: 'I expect to see you at all times behaving correctly and responsibly. I expect to detect a Red Squadron cadet not by the colour of his scarf, or of his name tag, but by his appearance, his courtesy, his standards and his behaviour. I say I expect it. No – I *demand* it! I demand it of each and every one of you.'

The Squadron Commander may have seemed rather formidable; yet easily the most alarming person on Red Squadron's horizon was their senior non-commissioned instructor, Sergeant James. A slim, wiry, dark-haired man who irradiated a feeling of great toughness, he had perfect timing and the classic NCO's turn of phrase: even though he never resorted to obscenities, he combined menace and humour so unnervingly that for the first few weeks his cadets hardly knew what to make of him.

'We had a good squadron last time,' he barked at them on the first day. 'I want a better one this time. No messing about. One hundred per cent effort is all we ask . . .

'A lot of people have come up to me asking about the barber's. For haircuts. Gentlemen, some of you have made the attempt. Some of you are not good enough. The good book says the hair on the head will be neatly cut and trimmed. My interpretation of that is short back and sides. No square necks. Got that? Short back and sides. The barber knows. I went to see him this morning. Myself. Told him what I wanted. Make sure you've got it by Wednesday morning – no later . . .

'My first responsibility is general discipline – keep you lot in line. I'll stand for no nonsense. No – don't try me. Get that in your heads straight away . . . I shall be on your backs for the first few weeks, and you'll wish to hell I'd disappear, but I won't. As I said, you play ball with me, and I'll play ball with you. Just remember, it's my ball.'

The first occasion on which the staff deliberately tried to make the cadets relax was the Meet and Greet – a supposedly informal drinks party held in the No 2, or cadets', officers' mess one evening after dinner. The idea was that everyone should let his hair down a bit, but, for one reason or another, the plan did not quite come off. For one thing, the students remained stiffly on their best behaviour throughout. Kitted out as they were in their uncomfortable new suits, they knew they were meant to relax but at the same time suspected that their social manners were under observation. In this they were wrong – they were *not* being spied on – but even so the idea inhibited their behaviour.

The demeanour of the ex-airmen tended to be artificial. On public display in an officers' mess for the first time, they tried to put into practice some of the rules of conduct which they had just heard about in lectures: the results were sometimes uncomfortable. One of them, Rhod Smart, gave a perhaps unintentionally clear glimpse of the difficulties experienced by someone making the transition. Asked about the differences, he said that lunchtime in an airmen's mess was not so much lunchtime as feeding time. 'You go in there, and it's every man for himself, literally. Once you come along to the officers' mess, once you walk through, you pick up your meal, you go and sit down. Everything's laid out nicely before you. You're looked after. It's a more civilized method of eating – and actually living, I think.

'Also, the officers' mess has the accommodation. While I was doing my training, the accommodation I was in was in bad condition – a sixteen-man room, absolutely no privacy, which is very bad, especially if you're supposed to be studying. Try and study when you've got sixteen other men around you. If one person decides he wants to play a record, puts the record player on, that's it: no one else is studying.'

The haircuts, so often threatened, proved traumatic, although even more so later than at the time. Long hair was then *de rigueur* for all fashionable young men, so to see the carefully tended locks being sheared away caused great chagrin and some hilarity. Yet it was not until the shorn lambs first went home on leave that the impact of their changed appearance was fully felt. Then families failed to recognize them. Girl friends took one look, screamed and fled, some never to return.

Another traumatic event was the first donning of uniform. For the first two days the cadets kept their civilian clothes; then, on the Wednesday morning, they were told to get up in their camouflaged combat kit, known officially as disruptive-pattern clothing and unofficially as jungle-bunny outfits. (Their proper uniforms were still being altered by the two military tailors on the camp, Moss Bros and Alkit.) The effect of the combat suits was startling: cadets stared at each other blankly, not recognizing the inhabitants of these strange garments as people they knew.

One welcome break during the hectic first week came with a visit to the RAF Museum at Hendon, as part of a crash-course in RAF history. Everyone enjoyed the trip, and found that the sight of so many tangible relics from the past increased the reality of their present.

Back in camp, what they soon came to call the 'buggeration factor' again made life uncomfortably hectic. Although there were officially five-minute gaps between periods, the cadets were often kept late, or had to change from head to foot, so that they were perpetually doubling from one place to the next.

Perhaps the greatest shock was to find how *tired* they were, all the time. Although there was no official reveille, they soon found they had to get up at 5.30 if they were to have everything ready for the morning parades. At night they had to work until 10.30 or 11 o'clock to get their kit clean, their uniforms pressed and their homework done for the next day. As a result, it was a great struggle to keep awake at lectures in the afternoons, and films, with their comfortable darkness, were even worse: as the lights went back on, the room would be filled with the rustle of people shaking their neighbours awake. Tiredness became the ever-present enemy. Whether or not they could afford to take part in some evening activity had to be weighed against the possibility that they would be too exhausted the next morning.

Much of the exhaustion came from the unaccustomed physicality of their existence. As Al Stewart wrote of the swimming, although 'intensely tiring', it was also satisfying because 'all the time you are going further than you would normally and calling upon reserves of energy and strength hitherto completely untouched'.

The same was true of the 'aerobics', the name by which, for some inscrutable reason, the RAF likes to call running. The aerobics test consisted of six laps of the running track, which had to be completed in a set time; and thereafter, whenever the test was repeated, each cadet was expected to improve on his or her own best. Aerobics thus became a personal challenge calling for ever-greater effort and fitness.

Preliminary runs, and the dropping of hints by the PT staff, raised apprehension to a high level, and the first test proved a tautly charged occasion, each runner being cheered on by everyone else. Nobody disliked the whole business more than Martin Oxborrow, who, because of his great antiquity, had already been christened 'Grandad', besides the more obvious 'Oxo'. 'PT, I am afraid, is one of my pet hates,' he confessed in his diary, and he 'suffered the embarrassment' of being one of the few members of the squadron who failed to complete the course in the time allotted. Trying to learn a faster pace, he was 'very disappointed' that when he asked the PT staff for advice, they only told him to 'open his mouth more'.

Drill, conducted by Sergeant James, was also physically demanding, but more of a corporate effort. Though some cadets were irritated by its artificiality, they soon saw its merits as a blending agent and a creator of team spirit. As a result, they became proud of their own performance, keen to do better and better, and in particular to see the other squadrons off the square.

Sergeant James, of course, was never satisfied with their turn-out. One day John McCrea paraded with a speck of food on his beret, 'You been feeding it?' roared the sergeant. 'Get if off!' 'YOU!' (to someone else). 'You look like bag of potatoes tied in the middle. Pull all this right round here. Do it now! That's better. What have you got in your pockets? A football, is it?'

'It's my wallet and keys, Sergeant.'

'You must be very rich to have a wallet that size.'

'I keep everything in it, Sergeant.'

'Looks like it . . . What's wrong with *you*, now? Permission to fall out and go to the sick bay? You got an appointment? You think you might be sick or something? What is it? Lassa fever? All right, off you go.'

Although Red Squadron hated their sergeant at first, as they were intended to, they gradually came to like and respect him. This was just as well, for he instructed them in many other subjects besides drill, among them weapon training, fieldcraft, camouflage, the elements of nuclear, chemical and biological warfare, and such homely matters as laundry and the care of clothes.

His practical lecture and demonstration on uniform

77

and boots will never be forgotten. As always, his phraseology was inimitable. The service dress cap, he said, should be worn squarely on the head, but not crammed down. 'If you start pulling down on the peak, it feels as though it's a vice on your head, and very soon you will cease to be part of the squadron because you'll be lying down in a dead faint . . .'

His talk on softening the leather of new boots (by wearing them in the bath) and spit-and-polishing the toe-caps had a classic simplicity: 'You may have heard parents, uncles, aunts, grandmas and grandads talking about bull and spit and polish – "Your boots will be highly polished." My interpretation is as mine are now – the ones I'm wearing.

'To get that, soft cloth or duster, a little bit of polish, little bit of water, and start working the polish into the toe-cap. Don't press on it. Wake up, you! Third row. Yes, you. Sit up straight. Polish. Water. The circular movement. Not much pressure. And after three or four minutes you suddenly think: Oh, look at that, it's starting to gleam – and that'll make you work all the harder. And you'll keep on. Water and polish. More water. More polish, until the gleam really starts to come through, and by Friday all your boots will be as shiny as mine. Definitely by Monday they'll all be up to that standard, or I'll want to know why. And it'll take a good man to think up excuses . . .'

Spit-and-polish apart, his advice on the care of uniforms was practicality itself. Since each service dress uniform cost nearly £150, he pointed out, it was worth looking after, and he explained in painstaking detail how to press clothes without scorching them.

Almost all the cadets reacted to their new surroundings in a positive, creative way. Though all were stretched, they soon began to enjoy the feeling of fulfilment got from overcoming difficulties and the team spirit fostered by inter-flight rivalry. If anything, it was the university graduates who had to make the greatest adjustment. In the past two or three years they had grown used to having almost complete freedom of choice: they had run their lives as they wanted, going to a lecture if they so decided, but to a film or a disco or a football match if that was what they preferred. Now, suddenly, ninety per cent of their freedom of choice had been taken from them; suddenly they were being yelled at on the parade ground, hustled from one period to the next, forced to comform to the RAF's programme and ideas.

Some felt that their intelligence was being insulted by the standard of the lectures, especially those on clear thinking and simple logic. Others were contemptuous of the rather crude way in which propaganda was put over, about, for instance, civil disobedience and strikes.

Also uncomfortable to the graduates were the lectures on social customs, several of which seemed to be about fifteen years out of date. The RAF still insisted that at OCTU officers should wear lounge suits in the mess on weekday evenings – and conservative suits at that. Even flared trousers were discouraged. 'We like to see your shoes,' was the watchword. The mention of jeans provoked a lively discussion among the cadets, all of whom had more or less lived in jeans before they joined up. Now, though, the lecturing officer ruled that, although jeans were universal in civilian life, in the services, where the wearer was almost continually on public display, they were not good enough. 'Don't throw your jeans away just yet,' he concluded. 'Do hang on to them – you may have occasion to use them yet. But generally, as long as you remain within the eye of the public or your colleagues as an officer, then you must adhere to a slightly higher standard.'

Another lecture which succeeded less than wildly was the one on wine. The speaker, a representative of Saccone & Speed, went off to a good start with a description of how, having had 'the misfortune to be at the wrong end of a night-fighter' during the second world war, he had come down in France and been rescued by a wine-making family, who that night happened to be bottling one of their casks. Later, however, when he moved on to a discussion of the differences between Muscadet, Moselle, Sauternes, Pomerol, Borgueil and Beaujolais, he lost a good many of his audience, most of whom were confirmed beer-drinkers anyway. Admittedly the lecture had the serious purpose of expanding social horizons, by teaching newcomers to wine something about the subject, and it was also the pretext for a party (a tasting followed the talk). But it did not seem to be a great hit on any count, for most of the cadets found the wines offered little to their liking.

One lecture which nobody mocked or disregarded was that from the senior medical officer on venereal disease. Initial embarrassment soon gave way to a kind of horrified fascination, particularly when the film showed diseased sexual organs. The tension exploded in outbreaks of nervous laughter whenever the medical officer made a joke, and the usual number of questions that followed the film showed the close personal interest that everybody had in the subject.

Part at least of what they really felt about their new lives was reflected in their diaries. On the whole, however, the journals made unreliable witnesses, for they were compiled to order, and their owners knew that they would be read – and corrected for spelling, punctuation and style – by their Flight Commanders. Thus the diarists were unlikely to record their inner-most private feelings: often they put down what they thought their Flight Commanders wanted to hear, and several of them would later look back with embarrass-ment on the facility with which they trotted out the RAF line on topics like unions and civil disobedience. They were also liable to make fulsome estimates of the way they themselves had changed. 'The amount I have learned about different topics, and about myself, is incredible,' wrote one. 'I am now thinking differently, aiming for higher standards, and beginning to think that there is a lot more to being an RAF officer than I had previously considered.'

It did not take the members of A and B Flights long to realize that they were both lucky enough to have outstanding Flight Commanders. Ollie Delaney, a university graduate, was exceptionally articulate, friendly and direct. John McCrea, in particular, got on well with him, and found the officer's close support invaluable all the way through OCTU.

In Cynthia Fowler, B Flight discovered that they too had an excellent natural leader. Small, dark, neat and athletic (a formidable hockey-player), Flt Lt Fowler enjoyed the advantage of having herself risen through the ranks, so that she had first-hand knowledge of the problems attached to becoming an officer. Also, like Ollie Delaney, she had a ready sense of humour, so that the work of the two flights, though hard, was always amusing and enjoyable. In the words of the instructors' manual, 'the OCTU flight is the microcosm of Service life'. Within this framework the aim was to develop the cadets' attitudes towards 'such things as mutual respect and trust, loyalty, teamwork, healthy competition, pride in service, tact, tolerance and community responsibility'. In this, Delaney and Fowler manifestly succeeded, for the morale in both their flights was first-class, and the spirit of rivalry between them just right, keen but friendly.

No discussion period generated more interest than the one on the role of the RAF in society, held in the middle of the third week. 'Is the RAF out of step with society in 1978?' asked the officer, and away went the cadets' minds in a dozen directions. People think there's virtually nothing left of the RAF . . . Their attitude is 'The Air Force isn't needed any more' . . . A serviceman is always that bit different from a civilian. There's something that raises us above a civilian . . . We've got a high standard of discipline. In civilian life at the moment the standard of discipline's extremely

81

low ... What about our politics? Conservative with a big C?

Cadet A: 'When I said I was trying to become an officer, everyone said, "Oh, you're going to talk with a plum in your mouth!" That was the standard reaction of all my friends. It was a joke, but they all think that RAF officers of today are still plum-in-the-mouth, stuck-up types.'

This misconception, at least, could be laid by statistics. The instructing officer had figures to disprove it. Between 1965 and 1974, he said, 5000 officers were recruited into the RAF. Of these, eighty per cent came from state schools, thirteen per cent from Headmasters' Conference schools, and only seven per cent from independent schools. The plum-in-the-mouth image is out of date.

What about unions? Why can't there be unions in the RAF? Chorus of 'Don't need 'em!' It would be impossible ... There would be no way you could have discipline *and* union interference ... Any order could be countermanded by a shop steward ... The rank system would go to pot ... The primary function of a union is to look after its members, and that's just what a senior NCO or officer has to do – look after his men. So in effect we've got the same structure. (It was indicative of the strength of the cadets' new allegiance that unions already seemed part of another world – the world of civilians, the world that most of them had belonged to only three weeks before.)

Back to the questions of rank and class. Are outsiders concerned about the class structure in the RAF? Cadet B: 'When I told my friends I was coming here they told me I'd end up alienating myself from them by adopting the young-officer lifestyle, driving an MG, growing a moustache, that sort of thing.' Cadet C: 'The pilot with his flying moustache, going out to fight in a Spitfire ...' Cadet D: 'I disagree. When I went to Biggin Hill my friends were all very glad for me. Needless to say, I got called a few names like Biggles, but it was all on a friendly level, and nobody thought I'd look down on them.'

Why does the RAF *need* a class structure? Isn't this where all social class is ironed out and people just work together on their merits – a meritocracy? What gives officers their superior status, then? Do they need it or deserve it? How should one treat other ranks?

In an increasingly permissive society, why does the Sexual Offences Act not apply to the Services? Why is it impossible to allow homosexuality within the RAF? Fear of blackmail?

To sum up: perhaps the RAF *has* run slightly out of gear with society, but only because it represents the more conservative side of society. Perhaps it is no bad thing to be a bit behind.

A final question from the officer: 'Have any of you got strong views on what has happened to your attitudes on the course so far?'

Cadet E: 'I'm very pleased that up to now you haven't tried to change our personalities, because a lot of people had told me you would try and change us to be ideal RAF officers . . .'

Cadet F (a re-coursee, who had been in for four months): 'I think it *does* change you, actually. I don't feel I've changed, but people at home see a tremendous change in me . . . subtle ways, so you don't realize it.'

Altogether, the discussion period provoked a valuable sorting-out of ideas.

By the end of the three-week OPC almost everyone had shaken down to the strenuous routine; but after four weeks one cadet, Jones, decided that he wanted to VW, or voluntarily withdraw. The RAF made considerable efforts to discern his real reasons. After he had first voiced his doubts, his Flight Commander gave him a week to think things over and told him to write a paper about the problem. Then he had him in for his VW interview.

Jones did not seem able to express his difficulty at all

clearly. More than anything else, he appeared to miss the freedom of choice he had had in the job which he had done for three years since leaving school. He said he found that RAF life did not allow him to express his individuality. The officer put it to him with some sharpness that the point of the early part of the course was to develop an individual's powers of self-discipline, and that as a potential pilot he would live a lot longer if he were self-disciplined, rather than having to have external discipline forced on him.

After some probing it became clear that he lacked commitment. In the end the officer let him have it straight: 'Well, I think there's a certain amount of mutual disappointment, because, quite candidly, from what I've seen of you in the last few minutes, I wouldn't have thought you'd stand a good chance of completing the training successfully. You're absolutely right: the degree of commitment isn't there.' So Officer Cadet Jones was allowed to leave. Once they saw how confused his motivation was, the RAF became as keen to get rid of him as he was happy to leave.

5

Officers and Gentlemen

The rest of the cadets, now joined by the OMC, soldiered on, on the one hand learning to be officers and gentlemen, and on the other acquiring basic martial skills. As they progressed further into the course, the quality of their accommodation gradually improved: after six weeks they moved from their barrack blocks to single rooms in a different building nearer the officers' mess (a great boost for morale); and after twelve weeks into the mess itself.

A constant problem was the close proximity of girls on the same course. The boys were specifically forbidden entry to the girls' accommodation block by a large notice, but it was an open secret that the ban did not keep everybody out. Nor could the staff prevent emotional attachments from developing: they might warn cadets about the risks of becoming intimately entangled, but they were powerless to prevent it happening, and several close relationships were formed. One of the most enduring was between John McCrea and a girl cadet, Sheri. No matter what the instructors might do to keep the two apart, they seemed always to gravitate back together. In the end everybody came to see that their relationship was symbiotic – each drew strength from the other, and positively needed the help of the other to get through the course.

If the ban on intimate relationships was impossible to enforce, that on the Bird in Hand, the pub opposite the camp gates, was even less effective. The official reason for officer cadets being denied entry was that airmen frequented the pub. If they saw cadets in there, it was said, they would start trying to take the mickey out of them, and there would be the risk of fights. A few cadets always defied the rule and slipped into the pub in civilian clothes. Needless to say, the landlord, Mr Whittish, could pick them out instantly, the moment they walked into one of his bars. Of course, he served them just like anyone else – and his good business sense was rewarded at graduation time when, for the night before the passing-out ceremony, his bed-and-breakfast accommodation was the first in the area to be booked up. Even so, he did not like the airs that some cadets gave themselves. As he put it: 'Some of these chaps come in with the attitude, "I'm a public servant," and they seem to have the attitude that you're a public slave – which of course isn't on.'

Another person well able to judge whether or not a cadet had it in him to become an officer was Taffy, the barman in the No 2 officers' mess. He claimed never to have made a mistake in predicting who would get through the course and who would not. He based his assessment entirely on attitudes and behaviour at the bar, and laid bets with his colleagues as to how many of each squadron would make the grade. Aggressive tendencies, he reckoned, were always a sign of bad character and likely to undermine the owner.

Mr Becker, the local manager of Moss Bros, was yet another who caught the cadets off guard. Not only could he predict the precise changes in their anatomy that would be wrought by the course (young men always put on weight, but hairies lost it): he could also forecast success or failure from their behaviour in the fitting room. 'If they come out with trousers on but no braces, all the uniform on top, you know they're not switched on at all. When you tell them what to do, they say, "Oh, sorry, I didn't know what you wanted", and all that. Well, I mean, if a chap's switched on at all, and he's going to be an RAF officer, he doesn't do those sort of things.'

The first major excursion from Henlow was for the eight-day camp, which was held on the Yorkshire moors, near Catterick. Essentially a toughening-up exercise, this took the form of cross-country expeditions, camping out, and generally learning to survive on meagre rations. The cadets were deliberately kept short of sleep – the immediate aim being to sort out the weaklings and moaners, and the ulterior one to prepare everybody for the real test of the whole OCTU, the six-day camp at Thetford.

Although at Catterick the cadets were driven hard, many ridiculous and enjoyable incidents occurred. Because of his outstanding ability as an athlete, Trevor Lewis was often chosen as his group's runner when intelligence needed to travel fast, simply because he could cover the ground quicker than anyone else. For an exercise called 'Dissenter', Cynthia Fowler secretly nominated him the group's spy, knowing that if he had to run for it he would outdistance all pursuers.

The leader for the day, Al Stewart, knew that his group harboured a spy. He did not know who it was, so became intensely suspicious of everybody. The group's task was to reach a particular map reference for a rendezvous with a helicopter; they had been given only one map, and Stewart, because he trusted nobody, kept the map to himself. In the end he managed to convince himself that only his Flight Commander could be the spy, so he ordered another of the cadets, Peter Kay, to tie her to a tree – which he did, with great embarrassment. She, though highly amused, of course pretended to be annoyed.

Lewis, the real spy, remained at large until he made an irretrievable mistake. Stewart had left the group temporarily to carry out a reconnaissance. Lewis had already managed to get the two strongest members of the party out of the way by deploying them as sentries, and was about to make his break for freedom. Then one of the girls suddenly noticed him looking at a map. Another map! Realization burst. Before Lewis could escape the others smothered him and tied him up as well. So Stewart returned to find his little army in chaos; the spy trussed like a turkey, with his legs in a sack, and the innocent Flight Commander bound to a tree half a mile away.

Soon after the return from Catterick came the mid-course review. First the cadets were discussed by the Flight Commanders and the Chief Instructor. Then each of them was marched in for interview with his or her Flight Commander alone. After asking the cadets for their own opinion of how they had progressed so far, the officers read their reports aloud, to see how the two views compared.

Of the television team, the one who came through with the highest colours was Alistair Stewart. Flt Lt Fowler praised his sharp intelligence, strong character, capacity for hard work and good potential leadership. She summed him up as a 'natural gentleman', with readily apparent potential as an officer. But at the same time she warned him against complacency and told him to work hard in the second half of the course. 'Think to yourself, "I've done well," ' she concluded; 'but also think, "I can do a lot better." '

Martin Oxborrow was told that he presented an excellent image and had proved an influential member of his flight, but that he needed to work harder physically and avoid the temptation to coast. He agreed with the assessment, and brought up his own lack of confidence in formal situations — something that had become uncomfortably apparent during eight-day camp, when he had been put in command of one of the flights for three days.

Like Oxborrow, John McCrea was found to be handicapped by a basic lack of confidence. Although 'particularly co-operative and industrious' as a subordinate, with 'a cheerful demeanour' which was an asset to any team, he had not yet realized his potential as a leader. The officers seemed slightly baffled by his character. One called him 'a terribly earnest individual'; another remarked on his 'ostensibly unobtrusive manner which conceals a strong and sometimes inflexible personality'. Perhaps the most puzzling feature about him was his almost masochistic habit of running himself down. Time and again – quite unnecessarily, it seemed – he would belittle himself and his achievements, remarking on how lazy he had been or how little he had tried. Luckily, in Ollie Delaney he had a Flight Commander who could get the best out of him and see through the slightly tiresome façade to the true worth behind.

Trevor Lewis's major handicap was still the phenomenal speed of his utterance: the trouble seemed to be that, just as his athletic body moved faster than most other people's, so his mind seemed to move faster than his speech could express. 'In oral communication,' his report said, 'Lewis tries to match his speech with his thoughts. Consequently, he is not readily understood. He is making a conscious effort to slow down his speech, and to some extent he is succeeding, but he must continue to work hard at this problem.'

The one really weak candidate was Rhod Smart, who narrowly avoided going on Chief Instructor's Review – that is, being put under special surveillance. He too knew his shortcomings. 'As a leader I get flustered if I think I'm going wrong,' he told Ollie Delaney before his report was read to him. 'I start panicking. That's my main problem – lack of confidence.'

The report precisely confirmed his own diagnosis. 'His confidence is improving,' it said, 'but he gets easily flustered if the unexpected occurs, and he is very impulsive under pressure . . . He still lacks the force of personality and strength of conviction to dominate his flight . . . although as a result of his efforts on eight-day camp he has established himself as a more credible figure within the flight.'

Altogether, he was told, he could not afford to fall back, because he was 'very, very borderline'.

Apart from the formal interviews, it was always possible for the cadets to go to their Flight Commanders with personal problems. The most difficult suffered by any of the group described was that of Martin Oxborrow, whose Scottish wife Anne-Marie did not like the separation enforced by his stay at Henlow, and turned against the whole idea of him training to become a fast-jet pilot. Obviously this upset him and impaired his work. He was therefore greatly relieved when she agreed to come to the Mid-Course Function, a special evening, including dinner, laid on with the express purpose of giving families an insight into what happened at Henlow. As Oxborrow wrote in his diary, the evening gave him a chance to prove to his wife that 'being insane was not a prerequisite for attendance at OCTU'; and it was a great help to all the wives 'to learn from an independent party /a member of the teaching staff/ the sort of things their husbands were up to'.

The second half of the course, everyone found, went very fast. As graduation day approached, the idea of passing out an officer became increasingly exciting, and the sight of Yellow Squadron (Red's immediate seniors) on their passing-out parade raised expectations still higher, for Red acted as the support squadron during the parade and spent many hours practising for it.

The work-load continued heavy. One exercise which proved particularly popular was the Office Simulator, in which a miniature station headquarters was set up and run by the cadets, each acting as a member of the staff, from Station Commander downwards. The aims were to teach them basic administration, and also to give them practice at handling human beings and dealing with their problems.

For the Interview Circus (a closely related activity),

meetings were staged at which the cadets acted as officers and were confronted by real officers posing as airmen whose wives were seriously ill, or irate farmers whose sheep had been panicked by low-flying aircraft. Often, to exaggerate teaching points, the staff would start clowning around, and it was all the cadets could do to keep straight faces and get the conversation down to earth. This was Alistair Stewart interviewing (or attempting to interview) Flight Lieutenant Delaney:

STEWART: Come in.

DELANEY: Morning, sir.

STEWART: Good afternoon, Fetherstonehaugh. Do sit down.

DELANEY: Fanshawe, sir.

STEWART: Pardon?

DELANEY: Fan-shawe.

STEWART: Fanshawe?

DELANEY: Fanshawe, sir. It's spelt Fetherstonehaugh on the board, but in fact it's Fanshawe.

STEWART: Fanshawe, OK, sorry.

DELANEY: It's an old English name and . . .

STEWART: Fine. Sit down.

DELANEY: . . . you know, bit of a boon . . . F-A-N-S-H-A-W-E.

STEWART: But pronounced Fanshawe. Fine.

DELANEY: Fanshawe – that's how it's spelt.

STEWART: Fine. Remove your beret if you wish . . .

The syllabus for the second part of the course covered a wide variety of subjects, including law, defence, current affairs, battlecraft, nuclear warfare and aid to the civil power. This last brought home to the cadets for the first time the nature of their new commitment. The lectures set out clearly what their position would be if they were called upon to help the police, and the conditions under which they would carry arms, and use them. They readily accepted the idea of fighting a foreign enemy, but the concept of acting in a military capacity against or between their own countrymen proved an altogether more difficult one to embrace.

Early in December Red Squadron sat examinations in Ground Defence, General Service Knowledge and Written Communication (known, like almost everything else, by its initials: WC). Yet the emphasis of the training was more and more on leadership, and everything pointed forward to the climactic final exercise of the course, the six-day camp at Bolney, in the Thetford battle area. This, everyone knew, would be a critical phase, in which their behaviour would be closely watched.

Preparations began more than a week beforehand, as everyone started to work out what they would have to do, particularly Al Stewart who had been nominated the camp's first Cadet Commandant, and was required to produce a full-scale operation order. The scenario for the camp posited that the United Kingdom was in a state of tension after a major incursion into Western Europe by forces of the Warsaw Pact countries. Most of the available troops, it was decreed, had been moved to the Continent, and RAF ground troops had been called out to help maintain the internal security of the United Kingdom. The job of Red Squadron – dumped out on Thetford Heath in sodden December weather – was to defend various vital installations, among them an airfield.

Although different cadets were nominated to lead each group on different days, it was left to them to organize their lives: it was up to them to set up and run the camp, get the cookhouse going and generally look after themselves. The main role of the directing staff was to throw problems at them. Many of these were designed to aggravate – one message, for instance, required everybody to shift camp in the middle of the night – and it was part of staff policy to keep cadets tired and hungry. As one officer put it: 'We're trying to lower their civilized, built-up batteries. We're trying to lower them down so that we get down to the real man, and he's not play-acting at all, but gives a true insight into his character.'

Activity began in the mornings at six-thirty, before dawn, and carried on until after midnight. The efficacy of the OCTU training showed in the way the cadets tackled tasks that would have been beyond them a few months back. One night they were told that an aeroplane had crashed in the middle of a wood, and that they had to rescue the injured pilot. In pouring rain, they not only found the site of the crash, but carried the man several miles to bring him to safety – a feat they would never have managed earlier.

Although the scenario was artificial, the staff's aim was to make everything as life-like and coherent as possible. Realism was increased by the presence of a Wessex helicopter, Phantom fighter-bombers and Hercules transports. All cadets got at least one flight in the helicopter, and for most of them it was a memorable experience, especially if they were deployed into one of the battle-zones by air.

The fictitious incidents devised by the staff built up in logical sequence to the final assault on the base camp. After it the participants all felt utterly exhausted, as much by the mental strain of being in command as by the physical stress of living rough with little food or sleep. Martin Oxborrow afterwards recorded in his diary that the effort of leading his group on the last day left him 'fit to drop', and that during the de-brief in the operations tent he felt that he was going to collapse. It was a tribute to his physical fitness, and to his all-round improvement, that he acquitted himself perfectly well.

If nobody actually enjoyed the camp, they were all profoundly relieved to have got through it, not least Al Stewart who found his 2½ days as Commandant extremely tiring. His nomination for the role indicated that he was in the running for the Sword of Honour (the highest award for the course as a whole) and had been on a final test.

At the approach of Black Tuesday – the day on which the results were announced – apprehension increased to a scarcely tolerable pitch. With so much effort behind them, and so much depending on the verdicts, the cadets found concentration on other matters almost impossible. (Strictly speaking, the day of decision should have been called Black Friday, since the following Tuesday was Christmas Day, and the announcement of the results was moved forward to clear the weekend. So strong was the force of habit, however, that the traditional name was used throughout.)

The long wait culminated in each of them going in – as for the mid-course review – for a solo interview with their Flight Commander. The cadets opened and ran a book of bets on the results, but this did nothing to ease the tension. As it turned out, Black Tuesday brought few surprises. Of the five cadets in our survey, the only one to fail was Rhod Smart, who was said in his report to have made a marked improvement during the course, but to be still 'below the standard required for commissioning'. Although he was judged to have 'a pleasing, popular personality', he was still immature for his age, and consequently liable sometimes to 'present himself as a gauche, rash and somewhat naive young man'.

Smart was re-coursed backwards to join Yellow Squadron on Course 332 and go through the OCTU again. It was particularly tough luck on him that, when the bad news came through, he was lying in bed with flu, already feeling wretched. He was not particularly surprised to fail, for he had been half-expecting it all along. Nevertheless, the decision was a severe blow, and not much mitigated by the news that he was to be sent immediately after Christmas to the RAF's hutted camp at Grantown-on-Spey, in the Scottish Highlands, for a two-week Outward-Bound type course of hill-walking and survival training. Officially, this course was designed to fill in the time before he rejoined the OCTU; unofficially, it was taken as a form of punishment for failure. The best that Ollie Delaney, Smart's Flight Commander, could tell him by way of reassurance was that a re-course was essentially a vote of confidence in his ability to graduate with the benefit of further training.

The other four all graduated without trouble. Al Stewart did not, as it turned out, win the Sword of Honour, and in comparison with the glowing praise he had received at earlier stages, his final report from Cynthia Fowler was a little muted. It spoke of his 'many fine attributes' and 'good set of personal values' and his 'clear, explicit speech' that demonstrated his intellectual ability, to say nothing of his impeccable social manners. But the passage about 'quiet reserve' and 'natural reticence' indicated that doubts lingered as to his capacity for leadership. Even so, he was commended for having done well.

Trevor Lewis's report again dwelt on the problem of his quick-fire vocal delivery. He was surprised when his Flight Commander described his way of talking as 'stilted', but she explained the term by saying that he had a kind of hesitancy, and placed too much emphasis on some of his words. She also warned him against being overbearing. She wanted him to be cocky, she said, but not *too* cocky. 'Don't lose this fight that you've got.' In spite of her reservations, she judged that he had reached the necessary standard for commissioning, and forecast that 'his quick thinking, alert mind and physical ability should stand him in good stead throughout his pilot training'.

The person who improved more than anyone else during the course was Martin Oxborrow. His genial, easy-going personality had made him much liked throughout; and in the second half, in spite of his domestic problem, which tended to leave him moody and preoccupied, he grew in stature and became a competent leader, even if still not very forceful. His 'mature and good-humoured approach' was particularly praised, as were his 'zest and effort'. Altogether he had sustained a 'high level of achievement'.

The main burden of John McCrea's report was that

he still lacked the confidence to match his ability. The many words of praise that he earned – 'industrious', 'cheerful', 'consistently high average' results in leadership, and 'natural ability to motivate a team' – were qualified by warnings about his unfortunate tendency towards self-denigration and his habit of hanging back watchfully whenever a new activity started, rather than 'getting stuck straight in'. This last was diagnosed as 'a function of his extreme anxiety to succeed'.

Long before McCrea's time the Directing Staff had identified a species of animal known as a DS watcher, which characteristically hangs back until certain that whatever it does will be seen by the DS in the best possible light. It may well leap forward when the going is easy, and skulk when things get rough. To some of the staff, McCrea seemed perilously like an example of the species, and after Ollie Delaney had read him his report, he gave him some straight, off-the-cuff advice about the future: 'All we've said about you is that you're suitable for commissioning, and therefore we'll commission you. But the learning process goes on, and the learning curve must be higher and faster . . . Life gets more complex.'

McCrea himself enjoyed the physical challenge of OCTU and felt extremely grateful for all the help he had received from the staff, particularly from his Flight Commander – so much so that the concluding paragraph of his final diary entry turned into a fulsome personal letter of thanks. 'The one over-riding memory of the course,' he wrote, 'is of the friendliness of the DS . . . My thanks go to yourself especially, and also to Flt Lt Fowler and Sgt James, although I can honestly say that I respect and admire every single member of our DS. We have been very lucky.'

Looking ahead to flying training, Ollie Delaney told McCrea that although general statistics could not be applied with much meaning to any one bunch of cadets coming through OCTU, 'if you do use statistics as chances, the chances are that some of you will fail. The ones who are going to fail are the ones who lack confidence and belief in their own ability, and lack the application to sit down and discipline themselves and work . . .'

The performance of Robbie Low, who came through OCTU on the next course, under a different Flight Commander, cannot be directly compared with those of the others. But since the assessments made were standard, it is not too difficult to see how he matched up to the rest.

His reports were excellent. His Squadron Commander, Squadron Leader Ken Clark, a fellow Scot, described him as a man of great common sense, highly educated, who responded extremely well to training and proved 'the ideal student'. The fact that he maintained exceptional personal standards was strikingly borne out one day when the cadet executives of his squadron carried out a surprise inspection of his billet: they found his bed space and kit so perfectly ordered that they singled him out for praise in their daily routine orders – a most unusual occurrence.

In the middle of his OCTU course some doubts crept in about his leadership: when formally placed in the lead, he seemed to abandon the principles of common sense which he normally applied to life, and became impulsive. This fault, however, diminished with further training.

His diary – which was franker than those of most of his contemporaries – often enthused about the immense benefit he was getting from the course; and at the conclusion of his final entry he wrote that he would be 'deliriously happy' if his name appeared among the successes on his own squadron's Black Tuesday. In due course it did, and he passed out in time to catch up with the other four at basic flying training.

All shared Low's opinion that OCTU had done them good. The physical benefit was the most immediately apparent: they were fitter than they had ever been. All had lost weight and gained strength and stamina. Oxborrow's physical adjustment was exactly that predicted by the tailor, Mr Becker: two inches off the waist and one inch on the chest. If the non-physical improvements were harder to discern, they were no less real: greater maturity and breadth of outlook, better powers of communication, both oral and written, a grasp of basic military and tactical skills, a greater knowledge of politics and current affairs, greater social ease, and above all the foundations of true self-discipline. For many – particularly those who had risen from the ranks – it was the first time in their lives that they had found self-confidence.

Oddly enough – in view of the ban on romantic entanglements – two of the five met their future wives during the OCTU course. After the Office Simulator week, which he had found rather taxing, Trevor Lewis decided to go for a night out in Dunstable; and so, in thick fog, he drove with some friends to Tiffany's, a night club. There he met Barbara, who had come with friends of hers from the opposite direction. Mindful of how airmen often claim that they are pilots, to impress casual acquaintances, he decided *not* to shoot lines, but nevertheless hinted that he was going to become an RAF officer; whereupon Barbara let fall that her father was an Air Commodore. Instead of collapsing, their friendship took off. In curiously similar circumstances, Robbie Low met *his* future wife, Sally, at a disco in Hitchin.

An impartial observer, asked to predict the chances of the five in getting through to the fast-jet stream, would have put them in the following order, and perhaps made the following comments:

1 Al Stewart. A smooth performer. Very much the Biggles type, with his moustache and MG. The best bet.
2 Robbie Low. Good brain, keen, plenty of potential.
3 Trevor Lewis. Boundless optimism and enthusiasm should carry him through.

4 Martin Oxborrow. A slow learner, but great staying power and good nature.

5 John McCrea. A slight puzzle. Can do it if he'll ever stop saying he can't.

None of the five was under any illusions about the difficulties that lay ahead. They had all cleared one big obstacle, but the ones still in front of them were higher. Ollie Delaney spoke to all of them when he said in one man's final report: 'Yes, it's the first hurdle, but you can't sit back and think, "Thank God, I made it." You haven't. All you've done is qualify yourself to climb an even steeper mountain.'

Graduation day brought the OCTU course to a fitting climax, both splendid and emotional. The weather was clear and bright, with overnight frost and an icy wind out of the north-west. From early morning the parade ground was the scene of intense activity, as the saluting dais was set up and rows of armchairs for favoured spectators were lined up with geometric precision.

Many families and friends had come down the day before to stay in the area overnight. Others arrived during the morning, and the parade began on the stroke of eleven. Afterwards, what John McCrea remembered most vividly was the freezing wind: he was scared that the blast would blow his hat off, or that his rifle would drop from his numb fingers. Yet, with its pomp and martial music, the parade was a memorable one. The hearts of participants and watchers alike glowed with pride, especially at the words of the Review Officer, Air Vice Marshal Tom Kennedy: 'You have now attained a standard at which no lesser person than the Monarch herself is ready to charge you with specific responsibilities as officers in her service.'

As the parade marched off in slow time, and the graduating squadron passed in stately retreat between the ranks of their successors to the thudding beat of 'Auld Lang Syne', and the scream of a fly-past by four Jet Provosts from Cranwell, many of the families were on the verge of tears. Many felt like Martin Oxborrow's father, who said: 'Although it was bitterly cold, I think we were keeping warm from inside, we felt so proud of him.' Trevor Lewis's father was no less delighted: 'He's our youngest son, out of six, and he's done us proud. His grandfather, uncles and myself were all NCOs, but he's broken the ice and made a commission.'

The ensuing church service sealed the solemnity of the occasion. The lesson, taken from the Epistle of Paul to the Ephesians, was smack on target: 'Put on all the armour which God provides, so that you may be able to stand firm against the devices of the Devil. For our fight is not against human foes, but against cosmic powers, against the authorities and potentates of this dark world.'

The preacher dwelt on the loneliness of command. To whom were the new officers going to turn when they needed help, as inevitably they would? When in a moment they stood for the Act of Dedication, and repeated the phrase: 'I will do so by the help of God,' would they say the words 'only because they are printed on the service sheet in front of you? Or will you say them because you know deep down inside you that they are true?'

After the service everyone relaxed at a grand lunch, serenaded by a string orchestra. In the evening, louder and lustier music took over at a dance, during which riotous horseplay naturally broke out. One traditional item on the agenda was the lowering of the youngest graduate from the balcony, where he hung head-down, held by the feet and subjected to a good deal of tickling, while he read out the list of graduating officers from that day's *Daily Telegraph*. With the help of such intellectual pastimes, the dance went on merrily until another frosty dawn had broken.

6

A Dose of New Medicine

Before the start of their flying training, the newly
commissioned officers were sent for a short course to
the RAF Aviation Medicine Training Centre at North
Luffenham, in Leicestershire. There they were issued
with their bonedome helmets and oxygen masks,
which had to be individually fitted and adjusted. The
helmets were stiff and uncomfortable at first, partly
because they were new, but mainly because the interior
cradles had been tightened as much as possible to give
the wearers maximum protection.

The student officers were also measured again in
detail, even though their every dimension had already
been taken at Biggin Hill. Once more, the aim was to
make certain that they would fit into the confines of a
fast-jet cockpit. Nor was excessive size the only criter-
ion that might disqualify someone: shortness of arms
could prove an equal handicap, for although the seats
in all fast jets can be adjusted up and down, they do
not go forward or back – and once a pilot is fully
strapped in, he cannot move forward, either. All
aircraft are fitted with a lever which does slacken the
straps to allow some degree of lean; but even so, arms
of reasonable length are essential, otherwise vital
switches will be out of reach.

Between the fitting and measuring sessions, the
students had lectures on aviation medicine and practical demonstrations of some of the problems that
would be encountered while flying. For the first time
they were made to think hard about the purely physical

problems of flying high-performance aircraft, and they began to realize what being fast-jet pilots would do to their bodies. For most of them, the new vista that opened up was a little unnerving.

After a lecture on normal physiology, the first specialist subject tackled was hypoxia, or lack of oxygen, and its effects both physical and psychological. As the lecturing officer pointed out, one of its dangerous characteristics is its insidiousness: it comes on gradually, without the victim noticing. 'The main point,' he said, 'is that it's not painful. You won't suddenly feel a stabbing pain and say, "Oh, that's hypoxia." In fact it's rather pleasant – like having a drink in a pub. You may easily feel as if you've been at a party and had a few drinks – maybe a few too many.'

Like alcohol, shortage of oxygen brings about a slight personality change, not always for the better. The lecturer cited the recent instance of a Hercules captain who was flying his aeroplane normally, but seemed in an unaccountably bad mood. The co-pilot looked round the flight deck, wondering what the problem could be: nobody was being lazy or doing anything untoward. Then he glanced at the pilot's oxygen hose and saw that it was disconnected. Immediately the reason for the bad temper was clear. Reconnected, the pilot at once returned to normal.

As with alcohol, so with hypoxia: different people react in different ways. After one drink, or a minute or two with insufficient oxygen, most people probably feel better able to drive or fly than they did before; yet the effects of acute hypoxia are deadlier than those of too many drinks, for they come on a great deal more quickly. This – the lecturer told the students – he would presently demonstrate to them in the decompression chamber, generally known as the Yellow Submarine; but first they must learn something about another possible emergency – rapid decompression.

In a jet such as a Phantom flying at 45,000 feet, the

102

pressure inside the cockpit is maintained at 25,000 feet – as if the aircraft were at the lower height. Should the canopy suddenly fail, the crew will move abruptly, in terms of atmosphere pressure, from 25,000 to 45,000 feet. In other words, they will suffer rapid decompression. This will make any gas in the body expand and produce sudden pains. Although gas in the stomach or large intestine can be evacuated, any in the small intestine may cause pain intense enough to double the pilot up.

One obvious precaution that aircrew can take is to avoid gas-producing foods such as beans and peas. But in this context the lecturer brought up alcohol, which also produces gas when it is digested. 'It's one of the main reasons why aircrew and alcohol don't mix,' he said. 'It doesn't matter whether it's whisky, gin, Ruddles County Ale or whatever – when alcohol's digested, it produces methane.'

Other places in which expanding gas may cause stabs of pain include the sinus passages, above and below the eyes and at the back of the nose, and the cavities of the ears. Any of these can produce pain severe enough to be temporarily incapacitating – and therefore dangerous to a pilot – during rapid decompression or descent. It is also possible that he may get the bends, or decompression sickness, a swelling of gas in the joints which produces pain in the shoulders, elbows and knees. Clearly, it is essential that he should know about all these possibilities, so that if he does get into trouble he can recognize what the problem is.

On the subject of alcohol in general, the lecturer sounded a dire warning. The point is that no two people react to it in the same way, either in the rate at which their blood absorbs it, or in the rate at which their body gets rid of it. The old rule of 'eight hours bottle to throttle' is therefore completely unreliable. Eight hours after a heavy drinking session, one may still be far from sober. Even a twelve-hour gap is not

103

enough. 'Therefore, do not drink at all the evening before you fly. It's a professional decision, and it's left to you; but God help you if you make a mistake, because it's going to be either your life or the life of the guy flying with you, or both.'

Another vital subject is the effect of g, the force engendered by manoeuvring in high-performance aeroplanes (the letter 'g' is used for both singular and plural. One g is gravity-weight, two g twice that, and so on). When a pilot starts pulling g in a turn, or as he comes out of a dive, centrifugal forces push him down into his seat, so that his blood starts to drain away from his head towards his legs.

To combat this tendency, fast jets have an anti-g system which, in any turn of two g or more, automatically inflates the crew's g-suits. These are in fact trousers with a system of air-channels running through them: they blow up hard and squeeze tight against stomach and legs as the pressure comes on. They are reckoned to give aircrew one g's worth of support. Yet even with them a pilot starts to 'grey out' at about seven g – a not uncommon amount to pull in a Hawk fast-jet trainer. Under that pressure his brain is so starved of blood that first he gets tunnel vision, as though he was looking out of the canopy through a tube, and then he loses vision completely in a grey fog (sight returns as the pressure eases). Pressure of that order also distorts the body from its normal shape. The skin and flesh on the face are dragged down, and the heart may be forced down as much as three inches from its normal position.

Life in a high-g environment is thus strange and uncomfortable at first, although people get used to it quickly, and their g-tolerance builds up rapidly with practice. Yet the stresses experienced in turns are small compared with those that take over if a pilot has to use his ejection seat.

In a relatively low-powered aeroplane such as a Spitfire, a pilot in trouble could roll back the canopy, turn the aircraft upside-down and just fall out. A modern fast jet does not allow any such easy escape. For one thing the cockpit is so small and so packed with equipment that a quick scramble out of it is physically impossible. For a second, the aeroplane is normally going so fast that anyone climbing out would be cut in half or smashed to bits by the tail fin. For a third, the aeroplane is liable, under present tactical conditions, to be so low that a parachute would not deploy in time to save its wearer.

Modern ejection seats are therefore guns which shoot the aircrew, seats and all, out of their cockpits with a tremendous punch. The difficulty for the manufacturers is to achieve the necessary acceleration without turning the human bullet into a lump of formless jelly. For 'zero-zero' seats – those which can be used at ground level – their answer has been to achieve the acceleration in two stages: first with a cartridge, which powers the initial launch, and then with a rocket pack, which takes the seat and its occupant 300 feet clear of the aircraft.

Even this two-stage system subjects the user to about twenty-five g – close to the limit beyond which back injuries may be sustained. The reason he survives the pressure at all is that it lasts such a short time – less than a second. As it is, he is liable to suffer compression fractures of the spine, as well as fractures of the arms and legs. His chances of being injured are minimized if he initiates the ejection in the right position, with head and shoulders well back against the seat, elbows tight in to the sides, and forearms across the lap (a flailing arm can be broken by the violence with which it is flung across the chest). Legs are drawn in under the seat by the leg-restrainers, and prevented from splaying apart by extensions that come out from the bottom of the seat.

Even with all these aids, ejection is still a hazardous business. To hit a slipstream of four or five hundred miles an hour is like hitting a brick wall. A pilot must therefore have the visor of his helmet down to protect his eyes, and his oxygen mask on as a shield against the 500-mph gale.

A film shot at high speed and re-run slowly reveals exactly what happens at the moment of detonation. First the soft pad of the seat is squashed flat. Then the skin and muscle and fat of the pilot's backside are similarly compressed. Then the trunk, including the backbone, is forcibly compacted. Only when all this has happened (in a few milliseconds) does the body start to rise. By then one spinal block has been driven up against the next, and some of the weaker ones may have cracked.

Having successfully parted company from his aeroplane, the pilot has the relatively simple task of coming down safely. A landing in water will be gentler than one on land, but rescue may take longer to arrive, and his survival may depend on the efficiency with which he inflates and gets into his dinghy.

To listen to this catalogue of possible disasters in the lecture room is rather daunting: it is a relief to go and try out one or two of the things that have been talked about. The ejector seat rig is a thirty-feet tower of latticed steelwork with a rail running up the front. One by one the students are strapped into the seat, and given final instructions about keeping head back and arms in during the one-second delay that follows their pull on the handle between their legs. Then comes the brief countdown: 'Ready? Prepare to eject . . . EJECT!'

Bang goes the gun and up goes the student, although only at a speed that subjects him to eight g – less than a third of the real thing. At the top each one stops and sits grinning, partly with relief and partly with pure pleasure, before being lowered jerkily to the ground. 'Great!' says John McCrea from his temporary eminence. 'What about another go?' The only thing wrong, as far as he was concerned, was that the one-second delay before blast-off seemed like five.

Nothing so violent happens in the Yellow Submarine

– although there too everyone is on edge, confronted as they are by a new experience. Wearing their bone-domes and oxygen masks, they sit in rows along either side of the cylindrical chamber, with the large, comforting, experienced figure of the corporal-instructor going up and down between them. Oxygen pipes and intercom leads are plugged in to the connections along the sides of the chamber; the entire system is controlled from outside, where the assistant in charge can manipulate the internal pressure to simulate changes of altitude.

The corporal announces that they will climb to a cabin altitude of 8000 feet, and then stage a rapid decompression to 25,000 feet (the sudden change is effected by opening a valve into a second chamber, in which a vacuum has already been established). The students sit grinning at each other as the climb begins. Only the instruments record the change in their cabin altitude. But then, as they reach 8000 feet, the corporal gives the countdown to decompression: 'Four... three... two... one...' *Clang* goes the valve. *Hiss* goes the air. The moisture in the chamber condenses into steam with the loss of pressure. Vapour forms for a few seconds. The students shift as sudden aches prod them. Now they are, to all intents and purposes, at 25,000 feet, breathing oxygen through their face masks and all set for the demonstration of hypoxia.

This is not immediately alarming, but all the same the insidious onset of the condition is rather horrible. The corporal tells three of the students to unhook their masks and breathe the chamber air while writing out their names and addresses with pencils on lined paper.

For about two-and-a-half minutes they continue to write normally. They themselves feel perfectly all right and do not realize there is anything amiss. Then, at two minutes forty-five seconds the writing of one of them suddenly deteriorates, growing bigger and bigger until it sprawls across the page in a huge downward sweep. Simultaneously, the other two start going to

107

pieces as well. The faces of the writers grow dusky, their nails blue. They are still making enough sense to obey the instructor's command and replace their masks, but they are not by any means themselves.

After only five seconds back on oxygen their faces are suffused by a bright pink flush and they are fully alert once more – but amazed by the sight of the writing they have just completed. They could have sworn that their hands were neat as ever while they copied out their addresses – a convincing demonstration of the necessity to be able to recognize hypoxia in its early stages. A prolongation of the oxygen-shortage they suffered would have led gently to unconsciousness and death.

Another disconcerting experience is the demonstration of disorientation. One by one the students are put into a blacked-out box with nothing to look at but a row of coloured lights. The box is set up so that it can spin horizontally. The instructor tells the inmate to stand by, and report what he thinks is happening to him; then he sets the box turning.

The sensation inside, though not sickening, is extremely weird. When the box is rotated to the left, anti-clockwise, and gradually accelerated, the inhabitant notices the movement and reports it accurately. But as soon as a constant speed is reached, and the acceleration ceases, he feels he is slowing down, and presently, while spinning at full speed, announces that he has stopped. Then, as he starts to decelerate, he reports that he is moving to the right.

For the rest of the group, watching and listening from outside, the spectacle is thoroughly amusing. But to go inside the box oneself gives a sharp warning about how the brain can be unhinged by unfamiliar sensations. Most pilots find it hard to believe that disorientation will ever affect them – until it does; but in fact a surprisingly high proportion of accidents are due to this very cause.

A Jet Provost Mk 5.

The five at Linton, photographed in front of a Jet Provost Mk 3: Trevor Lewis *(on wing)*, Robbie Low *(in cockpit)*, and *(left to right)* Al Stewart, Martin Oxborrow and John McCrea. THE YORKSHIRE EVENING PRESS

A Hawk about to be armed with rockets, bombs and 30mm cannon shells.

A Hawk firing SNEB rockets. BRITISH AEROSPACE

No 21 Hawk Long Course, Brawdy.

Four Lightning Interceptors.

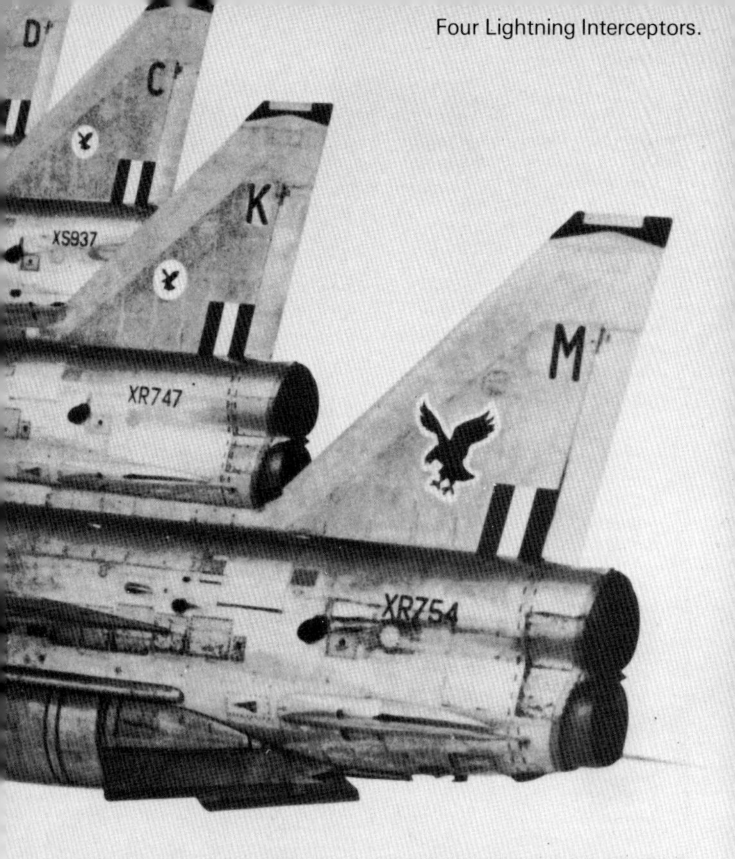
D
C
XS937
K
XR747
M
XR754

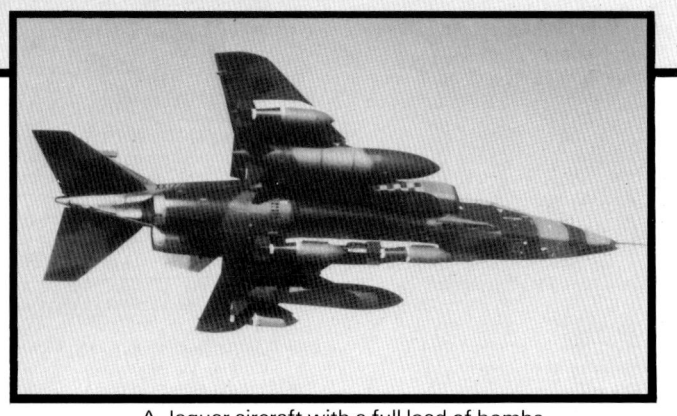

A Jaguar aircraft with a full load of bombs.

The pilot's cockpit of a Buccaneer S Mk 2B.

1 AC generator switches (port and starboard)
2 Undercarriage pushbutton selector
3 Landing and taxying lamp switch
4 Oxygen flow MI (pilot and navigator)
5 Arresting hook selector switch
6 Arresting hook indicator light
7 Stores jettison pushbutton
8 SWS attention-getter light
9 Attitude indicator fast erection switch
10 Compass card locking switch
11 Anti-dazzle lamp
12 Blowing system MI (port and starboard)
13 Flaps and aileron droop position indicator
14 Tailplane flap position indicator
15 Canopy jettison control handle
16 Anti-dazzle lamps master selector switch
17 Angle of attack indicator
18 Precision airspeed indicator
19 Location for stop watch
20 Approach index display
21 Terrain warning indicator light
22 Strike sight PDU
23 Undercarriage warning light
24 Standby artificial horizon
25 LP shaft rotation indicator light
26 Radio altimeter
27 Standby airspeed indicator
28 Standby directional indicator
29 Radio altimeter limit lights (three)
30 Accelerometer
31 Windscreen rain clearance indicator light
32 Windscreen de-icing MI
33 115V AC supply failure MI
34 Ice warning MI
35 Autopilot control switch
36 Wing blowing system pressure gauges
37 Standby altimeter
38 Engine anti-icing MI
39 Autopilot MI
40 Yaw damper selector switch
41 Anti-dazzle lamp
42 Autostabiliser channel selector switches (yaw, roll and pitch)
43 Autopilot ICO reset pushbutton
44 Engine LP duct overheat indicator lights
45 SWS attention-getter light
46 Fuel filter icing MI (port and starboard)

47 LP shaft overspeed indicator lights
48 Engine thrust meter and selector switch
49 Fuel flowmeter
50 Fuel remaining indicator and reset
51 TGT indicators (port and starboard)
52 LP shaft speed indicators (port and starboard)
53 Engine oil pressure MI (port and starboard)
54 Right rudder pedal and wheelbrake foot selector
55 HP shaft speed indicators (port and starboard)
56 Adjustable air-conditioning nozzle
57 Weapons release trigger safety catch
58 Control column

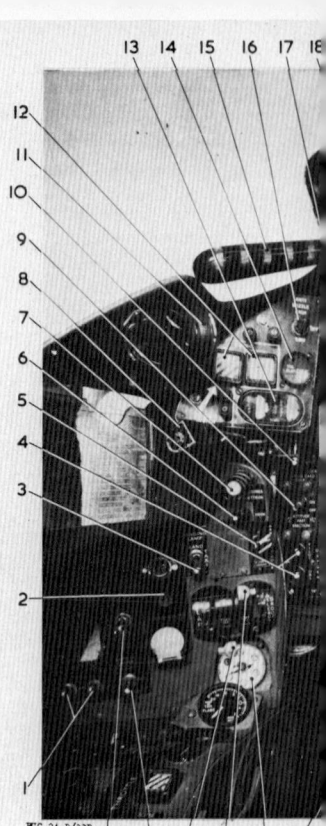

BCC 2A-D/33B

13 14 15 16 17 18

12
11
10
9
8
7
6
5
4
3
2
1

70 69 68 67 66 65

9
20
21
22
23
24
25
26
27
28
29
30
31
32
33
34
35
36
37
38
39
40
41
42
43
44
45
46
47
48
49
50
51
52
53
54
55
56
57
58
59
60
61
62
3

59 Weapons release and camera operating trigger (front upper trigger)
60 Autopilot disengage pushbutton (front lower trigger)
61 Rudder pedals leg-reach adjuster
62 Tailplane trim switches (two linked)
63 Autopilot ICO pushbutton
64 IFIS display, comprising:
    Airspeed indicator and machmeter
    Altimeter and vertical speed indicator
    Attitude indicator and slip indicator
    Navigation display
65 Left rudder pedal and wheelbrake foot selector
66 Undercarriage position indicator
67 Aileron droop and tailplane flap selector lever
68 Mainplane flaps selector lever
69 Battery master switch
70 Airbrakes standby switch

A Brawdy Hawk engaged in air- combat manoeuvres.

7

Going Solo

Course 37 at the Basic Flying Training School, Linton-on-Ouse, opened on 5 March 1979. Bent as they were on learning to fly, the seventeen students found it most frustrating to be plunged into a month's ground-school, with no immediate prospect of getting airborne. Yet there was no alternative but to buckle down and assimilate the vast amount that had to be learned by heart before anyone was even allowed into the cockpit of a real aeroplane.

The purely academic instruction included such subjects as aerodynamics, aircraft operation, avionics, combat survival, flight instrumentation, maths and science, meteorology and navigation. In all these the lessons had to be learned word-perfect, so that the pilot's response to any emergency would be automatic. In the sphere of aircraft operation, for instance, the trainees had to master, among many other subjects, the responsibilities of the captain of the aircraft; the procedure for escaping from an aircraft; the correct reactions to bird-strike, how to land in bad weather; crosswind limits on landing; how to deal with hail and airframe icing; and how to use the radio in emergencies. The sheer volume of knowledge to be absorbed was enormous.

The same was true in the CPT, or cockpit procedure trainer, exercises. These were done in two cut-out cockpit sections of Jet Provost Mark 3s, set up in part of the ground-school. First instructor and pupil would sit side-by-side, as in a real aeroplane; then two students would together practise what they had learned. Again, the list of what had to be mastered was extensive: how to recognize engine fire; what immediate actions to perform in the event of fire; how to recognize a flame-out (the engine shutting down); how to initiate a hot re-light; how to do a cold re-light; how to recognize mechanical failure in the engine; the drill for noxious fumes in the cockpit; how to recognize hydraulic malfunction and/or failure; the correct action for dealing with electrical failure; how to recognize a malfunction in the landing gear and how to deal with it; how to recognize and deal with a communications failure.

Twenty lessons were devoted to the procedure for start-up and shut-down, and to the basic checks that accompanied them: ejection-seat checks; strapping in; pre-start-up checks; start-up; after-start checks; pre-take-off checks; after-take-off checks; pre-landing checks; after-landing checks; and shut-down checks – all to be thoroughly memorized. Twenty-three lessons introduced instrument flying and procedures such as those for a controlled descent through cloud, a missed approach to the airfield and an instrument approach to the runway.

Besides all these there were lectures on the ejector seat itself, and on the Viper engine which powers the Jet Provost. At the local swimming pool the students were made to jump off the diving board in their flying gear to practise the deployment of their survival dinghies. A little light relief came with one of the combat survival lectures which was given by a local poacher, who put a lifetime's experience to good use in explaining how to set snares for rabbits and deal with any animal that might be caught.

Bored though they might be by most of ground-school, the young officers soon found that, socially and topographically, Linton had much to recommend it. The station lies in pleasant, gently undulating country only nine miles from York and within an easy drive of

Ripon, Harrogate and Leeds. The area is well furnished with good pubs and eating places, and for keen walkers the Yorkshire moors are easily accessible.

Like Biggin Hill, Linton had a stirring history during the second world war, when crews of the Canadian Air Force based there flew hundreds of bombing sorties over Nazi Germany in Lancasters and Halifaxes, several of them to attack the V-1 bases at Peenemünde.

Today, officers living on the station enjoy considerable comfort. Bachelors have large single rooms in the officers' mess, and live on equal terms with their elders and seniors. The mess is typical of many such RAF establishments: a substantial red-brick building of vaguely Georgian appearance, with big windows and long wings running off it. There are two ante-rooms, for sitting in or for occasional cocktail parties; three separate television rooms (one for each of the main programmes); a games room with table-tennis and bar-billiards; and an immense, rather soulless dining-room. If the food tends to be dull, there is at least plenty of it: breakfast is self-service – people collect what they want from the sideboard or from the kitchen – but lunch and dinner are served by waiters. The bar is well stocked with different varieties of beer, not least the local Sam Smith's O.B.J., and prices of both beer and spirits are at least twenty per cent lower than on civilian premises.

Everything seems to happen early. The cards on room-doors, bearing requests for morning calls and tea, mostly ask for the occupant to be roused before 7 a.m. Breakfast on weekdays begins at 6.45; lunch is served from 11.30 to 1.30, and dinner from 6.30 to 7.45. By eight in the evening the dining-room is deserted.

Many of the students are irked by the rule that everyone must wear at least a tidy jacket and trousers, with collar and tie, in the evening. They claim that the fact that they cannot relax sartorially drives a lot of people away from the mess – and as proof they cite the

111

fact that the bar is not heavily used, even though it is easily the cheapest place in which to drink for miles around. The sartorial argument reveals the great difference between the generations. To the senior officer, it is essential that standards are preserved. The presence of the students is a useful leavening of formality; but the formality must be maintained, and it comes heavily to the fore on dining-in nights. To the students, many of the traditions are pointless and insufferably old fashioned.

Little do most of them realize how lucky they are in comparison with their predecessors a generation ago. Protocol in the original RAF officers' messes was based on that of the cavalry regiments, and even after the second world war many rigid conventions survived. All officers, for instance, had calling cards, which they deployed in a precise pattern whenever they arrived at a new mess – one to the President of the Mess Committee, one to the Station Commander, and so on. An essential call, for every newcomer, was the one on the Station Commander's wife: dressed in sports jacket and tie, he would drop in – apparently on the spur of the moment – during the afternoon and begin to chat. After 45 minutes his hostess would offer him tea, which he would decline; thereafter he would excuse himself and leave.

At last the great day arrived for Course 37 to start flying. The aeroplanes on which they began were Jet Provost Mark 3s – stumpy little single-engined jets, painted red and white, with square-ended wings, and of considerable antiquity. Most of the aircraft were nearly twenty years old, but they had all been refurbished and refitted so many times that, in the words of the Station Commander, they had become like 'grandfather's axe, which has had ten new blades and fifteen new handles'. The cockpit alone gave a good idea of the aeroplane's age: the front of the coaming was

112

covered with a strip of Biggles-type leather, and the canopy had to be cranked open and shut by hand.

By common consent, the JP 3 was – and is – a pig to fly. Noisy, unpressurized, with the acceleration of a 'clockwork mouse' (as one pilot put it), it is unresponsive and demands constant attention. Indeed, it is said that a person who can fly the JP 3 can fly anything, and many students believe that the aircraft was deliberately designed in its present form so as to weed out all poor prospects at the earliest possible stage.

Typically, the morning which should have seen members of Course 37 airborne was one of thick mist, which made flying impossible, so that all they could do was to practise taxiing. Even so, merely to strap in and drive about the airfield seemed quite an adventure – especially as taxiing is much less easy than it seems, the aeroplane being steered by separate application of the left and right wheel-brakes.

Luckily the afternoon turned out finer, and a start was made at last. On that day – as throughout the first few weeks – the students took much too long to make all their checks. They found it humiliating to be struggling with checks and harness straps while their instructor sat smugly beside them, waiting, having finished his own checks in a tenth of the time. What should have taken them five minutes might easily occupy half an hour.

The first of the five to get airborne was Robbie Low, who went up with his instructor, Flt Lt Dave Marlow. The aim of the sortie was modest – a tour of the landmarks around Linton, notably York, the North Yorkshire moors, the A1, Harrogate, and the Knaresborough gravel pits – and the entire sortie was flown by the instructor. Even so, Low found it an exhilarating experience, in spite of the fact that he had been up in an aircraft before. 'It really *is* a totally different world up there,' he said after landing. 'It was very nice indeed. At last you see the point of all the work you've been doing in ground-school.' The other four were soon airborne as well, and the course began a programme of groundwork one day, flying the next.

In a Jet Provost, instructor and student sit shoulder-to-shoulder, with the student on the left. The controls are duplicated identically, with the stick rising between the knees to the right hand and the throttle under the left hand, so that the instructor can assume control immediately if he has to. The side-by-side position has important psychological differences from the layout of an aeroplane such as a Hawk, in which the instructor is directly behind the student. Side-by-side, the instructor can see the precise position, and every move, of his pupil's hands; but although this may be useful for correcting faults, it also makes some students still more nervous than they are already. It is very inhibiting to know that even if you make a twitch, which is stopped before it turns into a mistake, it will be seen and remembered. The members of Course 37 soon found that working in such proximity could have other drawbacks as well. One instructor had a habit of elbowing his student in the right arm if he did something wrong, and the success or failure of a particular sortie could be measured by the number of bruises discovered afterwards in the changing-room.

Flying at these very close quarters inevitably meant that students and instructors got to know each other pretty well. Each student was assigned to one primary QFI, and was taught principally by him; but if that man happened to be away, or teaching someone else, another instructor naturally took over.

Inevitably the students found it easier to establish a *rapport* with some QFIs than others. John McCrea, for example, found his primary instructor, Flt Lt Steve Pepper, easier to get on with than anyone else. There was an instinctive understanding between them, and Pepper did not resent the rather gauche and critical remarks that McCrea was inclined to make. McCrea's respect was reciprocated, and early in the course Pepper made a prophetic remark about him: 'He's a good chap to have around, and there's not much doubt that he's going to survive the system. He's got the wit and the ability, but above all he's got that certain something that enables him to think logically in the air.'

McCrea also got on well with Flt Lt Martin Coales whose merits (in McCrea's eyes) included the fact that he spoke his mind loud and clear. 'He's not one of these blokes who, if you make a mistake, doesn't say anything until you're back on the ground. He bloody well lets you know, there and then.'

After the first flight, the next peak of excitement was the first landing done by the student himself. This time, of the five, it was Martin Oxborrow who led the way. With Flt Lt Mike Jamieson beside him, he made his first landing on the afternoon of 20 April. After it, he was so excited he could hardly talk.

'I feel terrific!' he said as he got back to the squadron. 'That was the best moment I've ever had. Halfway down the runway – we'd actually hit the runway, we'd landed, we hadn't bounced or anything else – halfway down the runway, Flt Lt Jamieson had to take over because I was so elated I just wanted to scream. I still do!

'It was magic. I was concentrating so hard I didn't realize it was me doing it, if you see what I mean . . . I was landing it, and we hadn't bounced, and as we went down the runway I thought, Oooh, what about braking? You've got to slow down. So he said, "I have control," and I said, "You have control, sir," and he said, "What's the matter?" and I just couldn't say anything. I was lost for words, because it was magic. *And I brought it all the way down.* I never thought I could do it . . . Up there, at ten thousand feet, if you make a balls of it you're miles above the ground and it doesn't matter. But coming in there, it was amazing: I was so conscious of the thought, *God, there's the ground.*'

The excitement of taking control was a great tonic. If any of the five felt frightened of actually flying, he did not mention it. Yet, in the experience of the instructors, almost everyone is nervous at first. The fear is not so much of getting hurt or killed: rather it is a fear of the unknown, and of letting oneself down by not doing as well as one wants. But, sooner or later, nearly all the students did give themselves frights. As one of them described it, 'It's a bit like when you're driving a car. You decide to overtake at a particular point, and suddenly there's this bloody great bus coming at you head-on. It's only after you've done it that you realize what a close shave you had. And usually it's beneficial – it sharpens you up.'

John McCrea had one such scare when he was making a glide approach to land with the throttle closed. He thought he had positioned the aircraft just right, but in fact he rounded-out (brought the nose up) too early. Instead of sinking gently the last five or six feet on to the runway, he began to drift off to one side in the crosswind. He was still doing ninety knots – well above stalling – but his speed was decaying fast, and there flashed through his mind the fact that the engine of the JP3 takes eight seconds to wind up to full power from idling. All he could do was to whip the throttle open and hope – and in fact he made a safe overshoot. Had he touched down with one wheel on the soft grass, he could have been in severe trouble. Only when it was all over did he start to feel scared.

Later in the course, some of the students became anxious about particular activities, for instance low flying, aerobatics or formation flying. None, however, was as bad as a member of a recent course who developed such a dread of formation flying that when he strapped in for his solo formation sortie he was physically sick in the cockpit, and the sortie had to be abandoned.

In the same way, more experienced pilots sometimes develop phobias – fears which they recognize are irrational, but about which they can do very little – over flying in cloud or at high altitude. There is one particularly disturbing form of disorientation which can set in at very high altitude: the pilot is flying alone, without much to do and growing a bit bored, when he suddenly visualizes himself from outside the aeroplane. He thinks he is outside, sitting on the wing, and looking in at himself in the cockpit – a most unnerving phenomenon. Another well-known high-altitude hallucination is that of feeling that the aeroplane is poised on a knife-edge, so that the slightest touch on the controls will send it toppling from the sky.

Any pilot who develops a clear phobia is sent to the RAF hospital at Wroughton, near Swindon, where neuro-psychiatric specialists attempt to analyse and eliminate the cause. Full recoveries are often achieved by means of relaxation therapy.

Another problem closely related to that of fear is air-sickness. Years of argument within the RAF have failed to resolve the question of whether or not fear *causes* air-sickness; the consensus now seems to be that it can do so, and that it can certainly make someone already liable to feel sick worse. But the basic facts are that some people are more sensitive to motion sickness than others; that almost everyone is liable to be made to feel sick at first by the violent motion of flight in small jets; and that most people quickly adapt.

Those with a persistent problem are sent to the Institute of Aviation Medicine at Farnborough, where they are put into a hideous-sounding 'motion desensitization programme'. In the first part of this they are strapped to a spin-table and rotated, moving their heads back and forth as they turn. The aim – if the patient can stand it – is to increase the speed of rotation and the number of head-movements steadily over a period of three weeks, and so induce adaptation.

The second part of the programme takes place at Cranwell, where a medical-officer pilot flies with the patient in a series of exercises graduated to increase the individual's tolerance of motion. As soon as this is

117

successfully completed, the patient returns straight to his flying duties so that there is no gap in which he may lose his hard-won adaptation. The results are higher than a description of the process might lead one to expect: about eighty-five per cent of the patients return cured.

On Course 37, no one had more trouble with air-sickness than Oxborrow. The problem was not bad enough for him to be sent to Farnborough, but it plagued him on and off throughout his year at Linton. He also suffered another small handicap in the form of being left-handed (the stick has to be controlled with the right hand), but soon felt that this made no difference.

For week after week, through the long, hot summer days, the students slogged away at their circuit flying. At low level (where they spent most of their time in the air) the cockpits were steamingly hot and uncomfortable. As they soon discovered to their cost, flying is both an art and a science: to achieve mastery of an aircraft's movements takes time, practice and patience. An altogether more pleasant form of making progress was to lie out on the grass in the sun, learning up checks and notes.

A straightforward circuit looks easy enough on paper. All the pilot of a JP3 has to do is take off, climb straight ahead to 500 feet and then start a climbing turn to the left. He holds the turn until he has come round through 180 degrees and is facing downwind at a height of 1000 feet. Then he levels off and immediately starts to position himself for coming in to land, mentally, selecting his 300-foot point – the point in line with the runway at which, as he comes down the glide-path, he wants to be 300 feet high. By the time he reaches the threshold – the last phase of the approach – his speed should be down to 95 knots; and if by then he has everything nicely set up, he should be able to go straight in and land or do a roller – a touch-down immediately followed by another take-off.

It sounds simple. But several factors make it hard and harassing work for beginners. For a start, there are usually other planes in the circuit, flying round, touching down and taking off, all liable to make a hash of what they are practising, so that they need to be carefully watched and given a wide berth. The main problem, however, is the speed at which everything has to be done and the large number of checks that have to be carried out on every circuit.

A pilot lined up on the runway for take-off must do the following: select 100 per cent power, brakes off – the aeroplane starts to roll – look for 75 knots on the air-speed indicator, stick back, lift off, establish positive rate of climb, raise undercarriage, check for three red lights confirming all three wheels are coming home, watch for 110 knots and 100 feet, bring flaps in, check engine revolutions and jet-pipe temperature, look for 140 knots, take the power back to 95 per cent, trim the aircraft and look for 500 feet.

He then starts his climbing turn to the left, probably at a 45-degree angle of bank, depending on the wind, looks for his circuit height of 1000 feet, levels off, brings back the power to about 75 per cent, calls the control tower to say he is downwind and intends to land, looks for his downwind reference point (something on the ground by which he can judge his position), makes sure his speed does not rise above 140 knots, and runs through his downwind pre-landing checks, known as VAs (vital actions): speed below 140 knots; airbrakes – in, landing-gear – down; fuel – contents sufficient; flaps – central as for take-off; harness – tight and locked; hydraulics – pressure on, pressure off. Then he increases rpm to 85 per cent to counter the drag of flaps and wheels, trims out and lets the speed decay to 115 knots.

For the final turn in towards the 300-foot point he must lower the nose, bank, and bring the power back to 65 per cent, all at once. Round he goes at a 30-degree angle of bank, maintaining 115 knots during the turn.

Halfway through it he must check that his height is 650 feet. If he finds he is lower than he should be, he must increase the power and bring the nose up a little – left hand forward, right hand back, together. Then he has to check that the undercarriage is down – three green lights on the instrument panel – and call the tower again for permission to land, then make sure he is properly lined up on the runway. If there is a cross-wind, he must head into it, to keep tracking down the centre-line of the runway.

So he arrives at the 300-foot point, with 25 knots to lose before he reaches the threshold. Then: check no signal from the caravan;* select full flap; power back to 65 per cent; look for 90 knots; and, as he crosses the threshold, close the throttle completely, to glide the rest of the way to touch-down.

Since a whole circuit takes less than four minutes, the work load is high throughout. All the VAs have to be done in about ten seconds. Nowhere on the circuit is there a moment to relax.

Some of the tension of learning, as well as the close interdependence of instructor and student, emerges from this transcript taken during Oxborrow's Exercise 14, which he flew with Flt Lt Jamieson. Oxborrow's call-sign is Foxtrot 38, but there are several other aircraft in the circuit. At the start he is awaiting permission from the control tower to take off:

JAMIESON: Right. If we have an emergency, I'll take control. If I want you to eject, I shall say, 'Eject! Eject!' and out you go. Use the bottom handle. All right? OK on the approach? OK. Foxtrot 38 – take off.

OXBORROW: Foxtrot 38. Take off.

TOWER: Foxtrot 38. Hold.

* The safety staff in the red-and-white caravan parked at the downwind end of the runway inspect every aeroplane as it comes in to land and make sure that its landing-gear, flaps and so on are in good order. Verey pistol signals are fired when necessary: red in an emergency – if the runway is blocked or there is something wrong with the incoming aircraft – and green if all is well.

JAMIESON: Repeat it back to him: Foxtrot 38, hold.

OXBORROW: Hold 38.

JAMIESON: Don't forget the Foxtrot. What are we holding for? Three-eight – what's the reason for the hold?

TOWER: Not ready for you yet.

JAMIESON: OK. Let's just think about the take-off. You show me three nice safe circuits, and you'll be on your own. Don't feel there's any pressure on you, because there isn't. Ignore all the stuff you've got in your pockets and just fly. You've learned all the techniques, we've done everything else. You can deal with all sorts of situations should anything go wrong. You're now master of this aircraft, so you just show me you are master of it, and I'll let you have it. I've signed for it, but I'll let you have it. OK?

OXBORROW: Yes, sir.

JAMIESON: Fine. Good. Where's that other joker? Oh, he's down there on the downwind leg . . .

TOWER: Foxtrot 38. Line up.

OXBORROW: Foxtrot 38.

JAMIESON: There you go. What you can do is go slightly out to the right and come back on to the centre line. There you are . . .

TOWER: Foxtrot 38. Prepare for take-off.

OXBORROW: Prepared for take-off. Foxtrot 38.

JAMIESON: You can see where everyone else has gone – look. Magic! OK. Now, remember the order.

OXBORROW: Brakes holding. JPT 660. 101 per cent, oil pressure 32 . . . and I have been cleared for take-off. Releasing.

JAMIESON: Good. And use your rudder first, and then a little bit of brake. Now the ASI is reading, I shouldn't use any more brake.

OXBORROW: 65 knots. Starting to pull the stick back.

JAMIESON: Keep looking at the ailerons. *I have control.*

OXBORROW: You have control, sir.

JAMIESON: Now, it was a little bit nose-high, wasn't it?

OXBORROW: Yes, sir.

121

JAMIESON: Did you feel the buffet when you got there? You have control.

OXBORROW: I have control, sir. Brakes off, undercarriage . . . 100 feet.

JAMIESON: Now, if we want 110 knots, how are we going to get it? That's it, just lower the nose.

OXBORROW: 110 knots. Flaps up, nose up.

JAMIESON: What else do we check?

OXBORROW: 100 per cent. 140 knots, back to 95. Have a good look out first. Levelling off at 1000 feet.

JAMIESON: We want to be between those two big woods there . . .

OXBORROW (to Tower): Foxtrot 38. Downwind to roll.

TOWER: Foxtrot 38. Go ahead.

OXBORROW: Still 140 knots. Undercarriage – three reds, three greens. Airbrakes already in, 95 per cent threshold. Flaps to take off, and indicated. Harness tightened up – and yours, sir?

JAMIESON: Mine is.

OXBORROW: Pressure . . . pressure good.

JAMIESON: What didn't we do when we lowered flap?

OXBORROW: Check the nose. We've risen 200 feet.

JAMIESON: Yes, you've gone up 200 feet. We're too high. Just lower the nose. You're coming round OK. You're down to 103 knots now . . . Come on – 115. We're a bit heavy. Trim it. 95 knots threshold speed. Watch your speed. Come on – what's your speed now? We're back to 90 knots and we haven't made the runway yet. Don't lower the nose – just point. Right: *I have control*. What went wrong that time . . .?

After a temporary improvement for a few circuits, Oxborrow slipped back, his main problem being that he lost too much speed before he was near the end of the runway. As he made yet another approach, the atmosphere in the cockpit became a little fraught:

JAMIESON: Now, point, point. Not at the caravan, at the threshold. Not that. Put your tail up. Come on! Where are we going? You can't land on the green stuff. I want those lines underneath your backside. Don't be frightened to put power on – you've got muscles. You're back to threshold speed again. *I have control.*

OXBORROW: You have control, sir.

JAMIESON: Right. This will not do. All right? It will *not* do. You're just not listening. Now, think. Undercarriage. Flaps. Take off. You can't – I'm sorry, but you know we're both going to be sitting in the aircraft there on the concrete short of the runway, and if we are, you're going to be on your own.

Let me show you another circuit. I thought you might have hacked it on that one, but obviously not. Just relax a little bit. All right? Don't get so tense. You're making some stupid mistakes. You're not looking at the right things. I mean, Christ, your airspeed indicator tells you how fast you're going, right? If you want to go faster, move this thing. It's not the armrest – it's the throttle.

OXBORROW: Yes, sir.

JAMIESON: Move it, and don't be frightened to put on a lot of power. Here we are, look. I'm a bit slow in the turn, so I put power on . . . (*To Tower*) Foxtrot 38 – downwind to roll.

TOWER: Foxtrot 38. One ahead.

JAMIESON: Three-eight. Speed, 140. Airbrakes in. There's no point in waiting. Let's get the checks over and done with. Three greens . . . and 90 knots threshold speed. Now, aren't we lucky? Flaps to take off. Harness is tight and locked. Brake and exhaust pressure is good. Concentrate now on the flying. Trim it. Power up to maintain 115 knots. I'm on 1000 feet, 115 knots . . . 86 per cent, maybe, maybe less. Now we can concentrate on the flying. I've done all the bits and pieces, the nitty gritty. All the things are in the filing cabinet, so there we are . . .

Here we go – watch. Back down and left. I've brought the throttle back a long way. I let it stabilize, 115 knots, trimmed. No, it's going a little bit low. I want 650 halfway round . . . magic! Over the moon! Knockout! 650. All right. Looking for my 300-foot point, see

123

the speed starting to increase, I'm raising the nose slightly, look. Foxtrot 38 – finals – three greens.

TOWER: Foxtrot 38, clear to roll.

JAMIESON: Roll – Foxtrot 38. Now, I'm looking at my speed, my height and my 300-foot point, because I want to be there at 300 feet. Now, if I put the nose down I'm going to be low, so I'll put the power on – look – and push the nose down, gently. Now I can afford to bring the nose up because the speed is about right, and look – I'm a little bit low, so I put more power on. I can delay my flap selection until before 200, full flap. Look at the power I've got left. OK, but I'm not back to 90 knots, am I? It's slightly lower than it should be, but at least I'm not stalling. I'm nowhere near it.

Put more power on – no problems. I'm pointing towards it, and it's trimmed. It flies itself at those numbers – look at that. Beautiful stuff. See what I mean? I used a lot more power there, just to make a point . . . And here we are, on the runway.

Oxborrow was by no means alone in having difficulties: all five struggled at first; and John McCrea, for one, found the battle much more of an individual affair than the one he had been through at OCTU. Although he liked the people with him on the course well enough, he found there was very little community spirit. 'At Henlow we were working as a team,' he explained. 'Here you can't possibly work as a team. You're working as an individual, you're judged as an individual, and therefore if you're going to get problems, you're going to get individual problems.'

The place where team spirit did manifest itself a little was in the students' crew-room on the squadron – a good-sized, comfortably shabby place decorated by a succession of earlier courses. The inevitable coffee and tea bar was faced with rough-barked larch planks, and in the middle of the room stood a tank inhabited by two piranha fish. The small round dents which peppered one wall bore witness to the venom with which the members of Course 37, maddened by the monotony of the packed lunches made up in the mess, hurled their hard-boiled eggs at the plasterboard.

The other walls were decorated with large representations of the badges devised by earlier courses, or, in some cases, with the actual objects which inspired the designs. One of these was a flap from a Meteor, and another was part of a Jet Provost which crashed in now-legendary circumstances. The pilot was a Middle Eastern student who stalled the aircraft almost as soon as he had taken off. A full emergency was proclaimed, but by the time the fire-crews reached the scene of the crash, they found – to their mystification – no sign of the pilot. He, by great good fortune, had escaped from the wreck uninjured and had walked straight back to the officers' mess, where he was later discovered reading a paper. Questioned about the crash, he denied all knowledge of it. Confronted with his own signature on the Form 700 which he had filled in for the sortie, he said he supposed someone must have forged it. Undaunted by the recriminations, he later added his signature to those of his course-mates on the section of the wrecked aeroplane which was hung in the crew room.

For Course 37, the first big hurdle – going solo – loomed up towards the end of May. Inevitably the occasion was a traumatic one for every pilot: to fly alone for the first time, without the comforting presence of the instructor beside one, was another big step into the unknown.

Driving up to Newcastle in his MG to visit friends the night before, Al Stewart found himself flying circuits the whole way and using the gear lever as the throttle, because until then getting the throttle and the power-setting right had been his biggest problem. On the morning, he went out with his instructor, Flt Lt Martin Coales, and flew three dual circuits to make fully certain that he was safe. Then Coales asked him if he wanted to go on his own.

That moment, he reported afterwards, was an immense relief. He had been dreading a postponement, and fearing that the instructor would suggest that they went and had a cup of coffee to talk over the mistakes he had made. But no: he got the go-ahead.

The next few minutes were hell. He felt terribly nervous as an airman fitted a canvas cover over the empty seat and strapped it down to make everything safe: 'I kept thinking, did I switch anything off that's really vital when I did the after-landing checks? I had quite a flip through, and suddenly realized I couldn't remember any of the checks, and thought, Oh Christ, this is the final straw.

'Then I started having trouble with the microphone. I couldn't hear anything, couldn't transmit anything, and I thought, God, what's happened? All it was, I'd switched off the switch on the face mask. So once that was out of the way I could taxi.

'The point it really hits you is when you check harness. You want to say, "And you, sir?" but there's no point, because the instructor's not there. It's only then it really strikes you you're on your tod.

'When you get to the end of the runway and you've run through the pre-take-offs, you just bring the engine up. There's not a lot else you can do, other than just let the brakes go and zip off. And after that you start thinking, Fine – right you've got all the different stages in the circuit, and you try your best to do them . . .

'At the threshold I was about 50 feet low. Instead of being 300 feet, I was 250-ish. But I thought, Right, I can get away with it here. I think I muttered "Oh Christ!" or something as I was coming down the runway just out of sheer relief.'

Stewart's mates all gathered on the grass to watch him, and after he had landed they clustered round to shake him by the hand. The excitement and enthusiasm were the same with every first flight: for everyone, it was a great advance, a psychological barrier broken.

Of the five, only Trevor Lewis had real trouble breaking the solo barrier. The problem was his inability to land consistently and safely. In the circuit he was reasonably secure, but when he came to land he seemed to lack both co-ordination and depth of visual perception.

Because he had fallen behind everyone else, he was placed on Chief Instructor's Review – a formal procedure adopted with all students not quite up to scratch. Going on review meant, in effect, that a trainee was even more intensively instructed and closely supervised than before, but the term also carried sinister connotations. As Flt Lt Withers put it, students on review were inclined 'to get rather dejected, and think we've got the axe out and we're sharpening it to chop them'.

Most students on the JP 3 go solo after about fourteen hours' flying. But Lewis found landing so difficult that he needed several extra sorties, and had flown over nineteen hours by the time he eventually did go solo on 5 June.

With everyone over the hurdle, Course 37 celebrated by means of a party at a local pub. Supper was laid on, a competition was held for lowering yards of ale, and Martin Withers handed out the solo certificates in a festive atmosphere. As Ollie Delaney had remarked at Henlow, all the students had done was qualify themselves to climb an even steeper mountain; even so, the time was obviously right for a little celebration.

8

Difficulties

The first to go under was Trevor Lewis. Although he flew solo a second time, he then began to regress. He was to have flown a third solo, but in the fifteen-minute dual flight that preceded it, his instructor, Flt Lt Withers, decided he was not safe to go on his own. What would have been a forty-five-minute solo therefore became another period of instruction, followed by two more hour-long lessons.

Try as he might, Lewis could not improve. At the core of his difficulty was the defect twice noticed at Biggin Hill: his poor co-ordination between hand and eye. He could not position his aircraft correctly, especially when coming in to land, because he could not co-ordinate the movement of his left hand, which controlled the throttles and therefore the power, with that of his right, which controlled the stick and therefore the aircraft's direction and angle.

At first almost all novice aviators are confused by the apparent contradictions in the movement of throttle and stick, and by the effect which they have. It seems logical to suppose that on a final approach the throttle controls speed and the stick altitude, but in fact it is the other way round in the Jet Provost. To increase speed, a pilot must push the nose down, and to lose height he must reduce the power.

Lewis, in his own words, seemed to suffer from a 'rubber string syndrome'. Most trainee-pilots think of themselves as wearing a pair of gloves connected together by a string passing up one sleeve and down the other. Thus when the right hand goes forward on the control column, the left hand must come back on the throttle, and vice versa. In Lewis's case, the piece of string seemed uncontrollably elastic. Another problem was that he seemed to have no depth of visual perception, and could not judge what point on the runway to aim for.

Sortie after sortie produced little or no improvement. Lewis flew extra circuits first with Martin Withers, and then twice with his Squadron Commander, Squadron Leader Robbie Chambers, a man with immense teaching experience who at that stage had flown over 3000 hours and reckoned that he must have done at least 15,000 landings. On 19 June Chambers took Lewis through twelve circuits and ten landings, four of them at Linton and the rest at the nearby airfield of Elvington. Although the Squadron Leader professed himself reasonably pleased with some of the circuits, he was anything but happy about the landings. 'When we get near the ground, it seems to me you're getting tensed up,' he told Lewis after a sortie. 'You're looking at the ground right in front of you instead of towards the end of the runway. You're not really landing, you know: you're *arriving*. You're pointing the aeroplane at the ground, and when we hit the ground, we've arrived.'

In the ten landings Chambers found no improvement and not even any consistency: altogether, the landings were 'a ragbag of errors', and Lewis 'was not really appreciating what it was that was going wrong'. With great reluctance, Chambers said, he felt bound to recommend that Lewis should stop flying. Given unlimited hours, the problem might, he thought, be cracked; but since Lewis was still at an elementary stage of his training, it seemed certain that he would come up against an even worse problem sooner or later.

The Squadron Leader emphasized that the decision was not his: the next step was for Lewis to fly with the

Chief Instructor, which he did that afternoon. Again, an hour's sortie and ten landings, in perfect weather with the circuit more or less empty of other aeroplanes, brought no improvement. Every time, the Chief Instructor had to intervene to prevent a heavy or otherwise dangerous touch-down. 'I'm sure you realize,' he told Lewis during the debriefing, 'that none of the landings would actually have been safe unless I had taken control. So regretfully I have to recommend that at this stage you stop your flying training.'

To the very end Lewis naïvely hoped that he would somehow get through. He could not accept that his lack of co-ordination was a crippling disability. But at a specially-convened suspension conference, in the presence of Flt Lt Withers, the Squadron Commander and the Chief Instructor, his record was carefully gone through. The report recorded that his failure had resulted from a lack of natural aptitude, rather than from any character defect, and concluded that because he had the potential to develop into a capable junior officer, he should be offered training as a navigator or a transfer to the engineering branch.

In due course Lewis himself was asked to sign the report. The Station Commander added his own comments, and the file was forwarded to the Air Officer Commanding for endorsement. When first told of the decision, Lewis took it well; but later he broke down and burst into tears. It was a shattering blow, which at one stroke put paid to his lifelong ambition. Not that he harboured any resentment: he knew he had been treated with every possible consideration and that the failure was his own.

For a few weeks, while he explored the possibility of becoming an engineer or a navigator, he was kept busy with the mundane job of showing visitors round the station. Ironically enough his first group was a party of schoolboys, clean and eager in pink blazers and grey shorts, all mad keen to become pilots. When they asked how to achieve their dearest ambition, poor Lewis had to tell that he himself had not been able to manage it. In the end he decided to try to achieve another of his own ambitions by going to university, and so he left the RAF at the age of twenty-one.

Although the students devoted ninety per cent of their energy to flying training, they also had to learn their duties as officers. In this respect nobody kept a closer eye on them than Mr Holt, the Station Warrant Officer. An NCO of the old school, with thirty-four years' service behind him, Mr Holt was a tall, grey-haired man with a white moustache, a formidable upright carriage and a formidably loud voice. He had met the new course on the day they arrived at Linton, and he had lost no time explaining both his role on the station – that of general administrator – and his relationship to his new charges. His job, he told them, was to teach them their responsibilities as junior officers: how to deport themselves correctly, how to conduct themselves in front of airmen, how to pay the necessary compliments, and what to do if they see compliments *not* being paid.

He would be looking, he said, for poise, presence, and good turn-out; for self-confidence, good articulation, and the ability to command respect. When they came to carry out their duties as Orderly Officer, it would be he, Mr Holt, who would brief them. He would be watching particularly to see how they related to the airmen, not only on drill parades, but also on less formal occasions such as cricket matches. Moreoever, he would be sending reports about their progress to the General Service Training Officer.

Nothing escaped Mr Holt's eagle eye, and soon he had formed clear views on all the surviving television stars. He detected, for instance, that Martin Oxborrow must have had previous experience in the Service, purely from his manner. He described him as being 'of naturally clean and fresh appearance', but tending 'to neglect the minor details such as the length of his

131

sideburns and the length of the hair on the neck – two points which an airman readily notices and is quick to observe upon to his chums'. Although very competent, Oxborrow struck him as being too nonchalant and not having enough poise. 'He's big and strong, but his deportment on parade lacks that vital spark . . . he's too lackadaisical and casual . . . his drill lacks attack.'

Pilot Officer McCrea also had the necessary height and physique (in Mr Holt's view) and was meticulous in the way he carried out his own duties. Yet his manner was rather quiet: it did not 'really suggest authority – and of course airmen are very alive to this'. Flying Officer Stewart suffered from a similar lack of assurance. (The difference in rank between Stewart and McCrea was due to the fact that Stewart held a university degree, which automatically conferred greater seniority on graduation.) Although his posture and turn-out were good, he needed a little more showmanship and projection, 'so that the airman immediately realizes he is being confronted by an officer'.

In spite of his strictures, Mr Holt felt confident that all three would mature into good officers. The one about whom he had doubts was Robbie Low. Again, he found 'a reticence, a fear of coming forward. A young face. When I walk in the guardroom of a morning, a young face surrounded by the other young faces of the airmen . . . He doesn't stand out. He doesn't come forward to me. He doesn't take the eye. He doesn't announce himself. He doesn't project.'

Along with this reticence, Mr Holt sensed a reluctance to become involved, almost an indifference, that made Low's relationship with the staff difficult. Even so, he said he would give him the benefit of the doubt and see how he improved.

Chased on the ground and hard-driven in the air, Low and his companions found life an uphill struggle. Like Lewis, Low also went on review, after falling below acceptable standards during circuit consolidation. Although a slow learner, he was kept going by his sheer determination and responded readily to extra tuition.

The next casualty was the one who, of all the group, had seemed the most likely to succeed: Al Stewart. From the start of the flying course he had puzzled his instructor, Flt Lt Martin Coales, who found him a slow learner and slightly withdrawn. Nevertheless, Stewart went solo on time, and soon afterwards suddenly started to make much better progress.

To Coales, it seemed that Stewart's variable response was connected with events at home. His father had been ill for some time and in June he discovered that he had cancer. Obviously the news was a severe shock for Al; yet the fact that he knew what the disease was, and had spoken to his father about it, seemed to lighten the burden on him. As Coales remarked, 'It was very difficult to put your finger on it, but his attitude certainly did seem to change, and if anything he became more confident in the air.'

Stewart himself did not believe that his domestic anxieties in any way affected his flying. All the same, after that period of improvement, he began to find that he relished the idea of getting airborne less and less. It was not that he felt afraid: rather, that he was not doing as well as he wanted, and consequently became annoyed with himself. By the middle of June the strain was beginning to tell, and his frustration was increased by a spell of bad weather which forced the cancellation of several sorties. On 19 June, when asked if he enjoyed flying, he replied, 'Ugh!' and then went on:

'At the moment it's a hell of a challenge to get that aeroplane off the ground and make it do what I want it to do ... When you're flying circuits you've got absolutely no time whatsoever. You come down at the end of it really quite drained, physically and mentally. Invariably your flying suit is soaked with sweat, not just because it's a hot day, but because, even though

133

your body's not moving very far in the cockpit, everything's bloody well *happening* to you, and you haven't got an awful lot of time to sit back and relax.

'Sometimes when you've done a sortie, solo in the circuit, you come down and when you try to do your after-landing checks you find your mind's completely blank. The checks you usually know so well have gone completely, and you have to get your flip-cards out to see what you're meant to do. Once you've got the first couple, like hydraulic pressure and flaps, it all starts flowing again. But it's that initial jogging of the memory: the brain is so switched into flying that it takes time to get it back into checks on the ground.'

In describing how his mind could go completely blank, Stewart touched on a subject of vital importance. Every student found the same thing happening to him: he would become so overloaded with problems that his brain would momentarily switch off and give up the struggle. They all began to see that perhaps the most basic requirement of a fast-jet pilot was the ability to cope with a great many inputs of information simultaneously, to deal with every new problem instantly, and all the time to keep flying the sortie as planned. The instructors at Linton were, of course, thoroughly familiar with the way in which a student's mind could suddenly 'dump' everything, for the whole training programme was designed to increase the workload on the pilot, and therefore the pilot's capability, in gradual steps.

Like everyone else, Al Stewart had good days and bad days. The good days he enjoyed enormously, but the bad days became an increasing trial. 'The thing that annoys me,' he said, 'is the self-induced problem you have when you go up and just don't fly well.' He knew that his shortcomings could not in any way be blamed on his primary instructor, Martin Coales, with whom he had developed a close *rapport*: 'We get on incredibly well together, both in the air and on the ground. I trust my life to him implicitly, and I suppose he does the same to me.'

If anyone on the course claimed never to think about failing, he was a liar, said Stewart. 'That's the one thing in everyone's mind – the dreaded chop. It's bound to be a very prominent thing when you've got such a competitive type of course – not competitive in that we're vying with each other, but we are struggling all the time to maintain a set standard.'

Stewart began to notice that he himself had changed, something which had been apparent to his colleagues for some time, for he had become bad-tempered and no longer enjoyed a joke. The strain had physical effects as well: he started getting severe headaches, and although very tired, could not sleep properly. He went to the station doctor, who tested his eyes, gave him pills for the headaches and told him to come back in a couple of days. By the time he returned the doctor had had a word with his Flight Commander. The reason for the headaches, the doctor told Stewart, was his general tension. The best thing would be to take a few days' leave.

So Stewart went home. He found it a great help to talk things through with his family and friends, but when he returned to Linton, and had more talks with the doctor, he came to the conclusion that he just was not cut out to be a pilot; he had tried his damnedest, and things had not worked out. Not only had the pressure made him ill: he also very much doubted whether he would get through the course at all.

After much painful thought, he told his Flight Commander and Station Commander that he wanted to stop training. They listened to his reasons, but told him to keep going for a couple of weeks in case he changed his mind. At the end of that time, however, he felt the same and asked definitely to withdraw, setting out his reasons in a formal letter. A suspension conference was held, and a four-page suspension report written up. He was also sent down to the headquarters of RAF Support Command at Brampton, in Cambridgeshire, where he had a long talk, lasting nearly three and a half hours, with Squadron Leader Pat Hickey, a specialist in aviation medicine. Hickey asked him to analyse every sortie he had flown, in an attempt to find out when things had started to go wrong. He then wrote a report on the case and added it to the file.

Stewart was determined to remain an active member of the Air Force, and had decided he wanted to become a navigavor. He therefore spent two days at the RAF School of Navigation at Finningley, also in Yorkshire, where he flew one sortie in the back seat of a twin-jet Dominie. He came away much impressed.

In due course his file reach the Air Officer in charge of Training at Support Command, Air Vice Marshal Peter Bairsto, and he, unusually, decided to interview Stewart, rather than merely endorse the recommendations of others. For one thing, he wanted to assess for himself the impact of Stewart's domestic tragedy (his father had recently died); and for another, he was worried about the extent of Stewart's determination.

At the interview, he asked gently about the family background and was assured that it had had no direct bearing on the decision to withdraw. He then suggested that Stewart had perhaps been hypercritical, and had set himself too-high standards: plenty of people had passed out of Linton successfully, having done much worse than he had early on.

To this Stewart agreed that he *did* like doing things well: 'I like my best to be the best, or as close as I can possibly get.' When he said that he thought he was probably going to fail the course anyway, he was given a mild reprimand: if he did any more flying training in the Air Force, the Air Vice Marshal told him, it would probably be better to leave that kind of judgement to the experts. Later in the interview the point was made again, more sharply: 'If I put you in for navigator training,' said Bairsto, 'the question is, if the going gets rough, are you going to leave it to the professionals to decide whether you can cope with the course or not?'

In spite of the rebuke, Stewart impressed the Air Vice Marshal who recommended that he should go for navigator training. Stewart, therefore, left Linton, but not without deep regrets, for he had made a lot of friends there. What fascinated him was the idea that he might one day end up flying with one of his mates in front of him. That, he thought, would be 'absolutely super'.

His mates battled on. The scope of the flying programme extended steadily to include stalling, steep turns, spins, aerobatics, and simulated emergencies such as engine flame-outs. Gradually the students went further afield from the relatively small patch of sky that they knew. The three remaining members of the original five each found the going hard at one time or another. John McCrea, for one, complained that just as he had learned something, and was trying to master it thoroughly, he was always being forced on to something new.

The next big hurdle, the elementary handling test, came – or should have come – when they had each done thirty hours. (Robbie Low did not take his EHT until he had done forty-three hours, having had a number of extra sorties while on review.) The test was a difficult one, in which the students were required to manage the sortie for themselves. For the first time they had to put together all the elements which they had so far tackled separately, and to fly with a test officer sitting beside them but not speaking. Until then they had been spoon fed, yet suddenly they had to control and pace a 75-minute sortie on their own.

Low, McCrea, and Oxborrow all failed the test first time. McCrea's failure was marginal, and he knew almost before he landed that the news was going to be bad. The second time he did a great deal better. At that stage of his career he still found flying difficult, but at least he was starting to see what it was all about. 'The secret of flying?' he said in response to a question. 'That's something I haven't mastered yet. But I reckon it's thinking ahead of the aircraft. If you let the aircraft do what it wants, it'll do anything but what it ought to be doing. Flying the aircraft has got to be second nature, because you've got to be able to do it instinctively and think, Well, all right, what's going to happen next? What frequency should I be on? And so on. It can so easily get ahead of you – and then you're in quite a lot of trouble.'

For Oxborrow, his EHT sortie and failure proved a shattering experience. He found the silence of his test officer, Squadron Leader Chambers, most unnerving, and he was further disconcerted by his passenger's outspoken criticism: he would never make a Phantom or Jaguar pilot if he flew like he was flying at present, and he would have to improve drastically. By the time Oxborrow got home that night he felt 'very bitter' and 'absolutely destroyed'.

His discomfort was greatly increased by the fact that after the test the Squadron Leader had brought up the subject of his marriage, suggesting that being married perhaps made things even more difficult for him. By then it was an open secret among the members of Course 37 that Oxborrow's marriage had been going through a bad patch; and now, it seemed, the Squadron Leader had referred to the fact obliquely. Oxborrow was incensed, and could not see why the subject had even been brought up at that stage. But he was objective enough to realize that the Squadron Leader might be trying to provoke him to greater efforts. If he was, he certainly succeeded, for at his second attempt Oxborrow passed the test without difficulty.

A welcome break from the grind of flying-training came in the form of the LSE, or Leadership Survival Exercise, in which, for four days, the students were dumped out on the Yorkshire moors and encouraged to fend for themselves. The threat of sudden survival exercises was ever-present at Linton, for there, as at many other RAF stations, the staff every now and then staged a 'gotcha', in which aircrew were snatched as they came in from a sortie and driven straight out on to the moors. They would be abandoned there for twenty-four hours – the aim being to ensure that everyone habitually wore plenty of clothes, such as sweaters and long-johns, under their flying suits.

The LSE, however, was a more highly organized and planned expedition, beginning with an eight-mile march to simulate ejection shock. For four nights the students slept out, in tepees made out of parachutes, and learned such invaluable secrets as that the best way of keeping warm at night is not to build a fire and go to bed beside it, but to heat a large stone or brick in the fire and take that to bed with you.

The Directing Staff provided no food except some live chickens (supplied, incidentally, by one of the QFIs). A distressing scene took place when the students tried to kill one of the live offerings. They had already been given a demonstration of how to wring the chicken's neck, but although they bent its head right back, they failed to do it properly and the wretched bird escaped squawking across the moors with everyone in pursuit. It took John McCrea, with his practical farming background, to give it the *coup de grâce*.

Night moves, orientation marches, escape and evasion exercises – for five days the students got little respite. The point – as Group Captain Robert Wood, the Station Commander at Linton put it – was that they should not merely get through the exercise, but that they should set out to beat it positively and survive with spirit.

Back at Linton they went on to night-flying – something that Oxborrow, in particular, found fascinating. 'We went up at about half-past two in the morning,' he reported. 'The moon was out, and it was

139

absolutely glorious. A bit scary, too. If you get between layers of cloud you can't tell where the horizon is . . . It would be very easy to get completely disorientated. Landing was scary, too. Although you can see the lights, you can't actually see the runway. There's a tendency to round-out /bring the nose up for landing/ much too high, and then of course you flop down and sort of crash in − and get a nudge in the side and a bellow in the ear from your instructor.'

Soon night-flying was popular with everyone, and the most coveted flying wave of all was the one which went off just at dusk, when the scent of mown grass hung in the thickening air. The trick was to chase the setting sun: having enjoyed one sunset on the ground, the pilot would climb up to another and another and another, until he ran out of height around 20,000 feet. From up there, in clear weather, he would be able to survey the lights of Birkenhead and other towns on the opposite side of England, and then he would descend into the moonlit blackness of the world below.

With their advancing skills, the students were able to fly in worse weather than before. Navigation exercises began teaching them to find their way round the country, and they became aware of the problems caused by low-flying, which does not exactly endear the RAF to the civilian population.

At this stage of their careers the three remaining members of the television team were all of average ability or slightly below. But Course 37 did contain some students of greater ability as pilots, notably Paul Field, a university graduate with a degree in physics who had already flown nearly 200 hours on Bulldog trainers with his university air squadron. He, naturally, had a great advantage over the beginners. Whereas he was already flying instinctively and had time to consider whatever new tasks a sortie might entail, the late starters had to devote most of their brainpower to the basic task of keeping the aircraft where they wanted it.

Another   outstanding   personality   was   Louis

McQuade, who had been to school in Kenya and had got a private pilot's licence there. So aggressive was he, in both his behaviour and his flying, that his colleagues nicknamed him 'The Beast', but everyone acknowledged that his motivation towards fast jets was exceptionally strong.

The syllabus steadily extended to include more difficult tasks such as the use of navigational beacons, route-planning and formation-flying. For instrument-flying lessons the students had dark visors lowered over their faces so that they could not see out through the canopy – a piece of training that at first brought some of them to the verge of panic. In aerobatics and tail-chases they learned to fly harder and harder, until they were pulling $5\frac{1}{2}$ g, the limit set for the Jet Provost. At that pressure they started to grey out, for the aeroplane has no anti-gravity system to support the pilot. Their reports began to speak of them flying not merely with or without precision, but with or without spirit and attack.

For Low, McCrea and Oxborrow, life seemed to become a succession of ever-higher obstacles, and all were on review at one stage or another. Nevertheless, they all managed to get through the basic handling test in September. The final handling test, at the end of October, almost proved John McCrea's undoing. He failed at the first attempt, and again at the second, which was wrecked by bad weather. He thus fell behind the rest of his friends, who had finished their 100-hour course on the Jet Provost Mark 3 and had progressed to the faster and more powerful Mark 5. He knew that if he failed his FHT for the third time, he might well be dropped from flying training altogether.

His life seemed to have reached a low ebb. He felt miserable anyway, for he and his girlfriend Sheri had just parted company. And he had hoped to pass the FHT without difficulty, so failure had been a further unpleasant surprise. As his instructor Steve Pepper put it: 'He's miserable as sin at the moment; his mental attitude is bad, and that's why he failed.'

McCrea himself realized that he was below his best and went to the medical officer for advice because he felt so exhausted. The tiredness, he said, seemed to have crept up on him, and now he was so weary that he could no longer do the things he had been able to do so easily before. He found it hard to concentrate while flying, and his brain had become blurred. He attributed the exhaustion to the fact that he had had no more than two consecutive days' leave since the beginning of March.

It was typical of McCrea's blunt, outspoken nature that he brought the matter up – to the considerable embarrassment of the senior officers at Linton – when Mr Geoffrey Pattie, the Under-Secretary of State for Defence, made an official visit to the station on 28 November. The students were in fact invited to raise points for discussion, and McCrea did not hesitate to lead the way: 'As a direct entrant from civilian life, one of the things that attracted me to the RAF was the prospect of six weeks' annual leave. I have just finished a leave year now, and in that year I got two weeks . . .'

The question provoked some bland answers about the difficulties of fitting everything in to the time available, and did nothing to endear McCrea to the authorities. Nevertheless, on the following day, 29 November, he did at last pass his FHT, graduating to the Mark 5 along with the others. Moreover, whether by coincidence or not, the whole of the course enjoyed leave the following week.

All found the new aeroplane an enormous improvement, particularly Oxborrow who described his first trip in one as 'Terrific! When this one makes a noise, it goes faster! When you open the throttle, something happens. Today we were doing 350 knots, and everything was smooth and quiet, whereas in the Mark 3 you'd be bumping around, deafened by this clanging

142

noise behind you. The Five feels nicer on the stick – it's like driving a sports car after a lorry.'

Enthusiastic though he might be, Oxborrow was in severe trouble at home. His marriage had almost broken down: he and his wife had decided to separate, and he was making preparations for a move back into the officers' mess. In a way it was a relief to have taken the decision, but he still felt confused and guilty about what had happened. On the one hand he thought Anne-Marie had not given him the support he might have expected: she had never really wanted him to fly, and had made that clear. On the other hand, he felt that he himself had perhaps been selfish to put his career before his home life: what he really wanted was to win his wings, and nothing was going to get in the way of that ambition. Was that callous, he wondered, or just realistic? In any event, he and Anne-Marie had decided that the only thing to do was to split up.

By the time Course 37 graduated to the Mark 5, a Role Disposal Board had already sat to sketch out a provisional future for each student. Representatives of the Command Staff and the Advanced Flying Training Schools joined the Linton instructors to assess the merits of every individual.

Officers who themselves had flown helicopters or multi-engined aeroplanes hastened to point out – not least to the students themselves – that it was no disgrace to be chosen for either of these types. Fast-jet pilots are not necessarily the *best* pilots, they said: they are merely different, and have different kinds of skills. All the same, among the students the feeling persisted that fast jets were the highest form of challenge, and this was reflected in the choice of aeroplane that everyone put down. Most said they would like to fly Tornados, Harriers, Jaguars, Phantoms, or Lightnings; and many put helicopters, rather than multi-engined aircraft, as their second choice. The students' wishes were naturally taken into account when the Role Disposal Board discussed their future, but in practice

143

a great deal depended on the availability of slots, and on the numbers of pilots that would be needed for particular types of aircraft in fifteen months' time.

Both Low and McCrea were judged good enough to carry on into Group One, Phase One – the first part of the advanced training, which in due course they would continue at Valley. Oxborrow was also assigned to Group One, Phase One, but with a proviso: the Board was not confident that he would reach a high enough standard to go on to Valley, and suggested that he might be more suitable for multi-engined aircraft.

This, it turned out, was an accurate diagnosis. Though Oxborrow did complete the 60-hour Mark 5 course, and passed his final handling test at the second attempt, he was not recommended for fast jets. The staff felt that he was not entirely happy with high-speed, high-g manoeuvres, and not at home in the strenuous physical environment of fast-jet operation. The decision came as no surprise to him, for he had long since decided that he would prefer to fly helicopters, and he had been dreading the idea of going to Valley. When Squadron Leader Chambers told him the worst, it was as much as he could do to stop himself smiling with relief. He did just manage to preserve the appearance of a disappointed aviator, and soon this proved appropriate, for he was posted not to helicopters but to multi-engine training.

The Board's decision brought him further domestic problems, although of a more pleasant nature than many earlier ones. After another crisis, he and Anne-Marie had gone back together (he had never actually moved back into the officers' mess) and, jumping the gun, they had already arranged to take over a married quarter at Valley. Their furniture was on the point of being moved up there. To unravel the arrangements at the last moment was a nuisance, but Anne-Marie did not mind in the least: on the contrary, she was delighted that Martin was not going on to fast jets after all. Beside that major relief, minor organizational upsets were as nothing.

McCrea scraped through to Valley, but not with much to spare. According to the Chief Instructor at Linton, Wing Commander John Lunt, he 'satisfied the course minimum standards ... but we think he is rather a training risk, and we aren't confident at this stage that he'll pass the Valley course'. That was not to say he expected McCrea to fail – far from it: 'Many students about whom we've had doubts have proved us wrong ... Suddenly everything seems to click into place, and they start to accelerate.'

Of the three, the one who really came good at Linton was Robbie Low. Although he had struggled at first, he later improved so much that he achieved a perfectly acceptable standard, and indeed was runner-up in the aerobatics competition. His final report was excellent: apart from slight criticism of his reluctance to hold position in close-formation flying, it was almost all praise for his exceptional enthusiasm and determination. He clearly enjoyed Linton more than many of his contemporaries, and by the end of the course his flying was described as 'spirited'.

'You need have no worries,' his Squadron Commander told him. 'You're a jolly good candidate for Valley. But you're going to have to work hard there. Here we treat you with kid gloves ... There, you'll have to be more self-reliant and determined, and decide when to do things off your own bat.'

Because the weather in February was so atrocious, the end of Course 37's programme was delayed. Open Day, which should have marked its finish, was in fact held while there was still a week's work to be done. All the same, the awards were presented as usual, and in his speech after lunch (to which families had been invited) Squadron Leader Chambers announced the prize winners.

The award for the best progress in the basic phase of flying went to Bill Harrison, an outstanding pilot who later became a creamy and returned to Linton as an instructor. The prize for the best all-round performance in the basic phase was won by Paul Field, who was also runner-up for two other awards. Special mention was made of Louis McQuade, who had been appointed Senior Officer for the last part of the course and had done an outstanding job in the tiresome administrative role. (He was also said to have been banned from every Chinese restaurant in York, having criticized the smell in one of them.)

Thus by March 1980 four of the six selected together at Biggin Hill had fallen out of the fast-jet stream, and only two, Robbie Low and John McCrea, went on to advanced flying training in Anglesey. If anyone had laid bets according to the form chart drawn up at the end of OCTU, he would have lost most, if not all, of his money.

9

Fast and Low

Together with nine others, Low and McCrea joined Course 45 at the Advanced Flying School, Valley, at the end of March 1980 for twenty-one weeks of training on the Hawk. Everyone arrived there in a state of some anxiety, for Valley's reputation was formidable. It was a hard place, people said, where the chances of being chopped were very high.

Certainly the station is about as far from civilization as it is possible to be in the United Kingdom – on the north-western extremity of Anglesey, and only a couple of miles from the end of the road at Holyhead. The main reason for having a training base in such an inaccessible spot is meteorological: the weather is exceptionally good. Snow is almost unknown, and the airfield is rarely closed by fog or low cloud. For this reason Valley is a master diversion airfield, open twenty-four hours a day throughout the year to receive aircraft, military or civilian, that have been unable to land elsewhere. The officers' mess holds a stock of diversion kits, containing toothbrush, shaving gear and pyjamas, for pilots who seek refuge overnight.

The airfield is a busy one, for besides the Advanced Flying School it houses the Hawk element of the Central Flying School, which trains already-qualified pilots to become instructors, the search-and-rescue training squadron, one flight of search-and-rescue helicopters from 22 Squadron, and also the Strike Command Air-to-Air Missile Establishment.

The star of the station, for instructors and students

alike, is the Hawk trainer, here painted red and white
to make it as conspicuous as possible. A neat, handy
modern aeroplane designed to the RAF's own speci-
fications, the Hawk was brought into service only six
years ago. Visitors from far and wide come to Valley to
look at the RAF's training system, and British Aerospace, makers of the Hawk, send prospective customers
there from all over the world to see the aeroplane in
action. 'Fortunately, we think it's a winner,' said the
Station Commander, Group Captain Alan Blackley, 'so
it's no bother to us to crack it up. French, Japanese,
Israelis, Saudis, Nigerians, Americans, Australians –
we fly them all.'

For the students of Course 45 who had just left the
Jet Provost, the Hawk was a revelation, and the tedium
of ground-school – the first five weeks of the Valley
course – was banished by a familiarization trip with
an instructor. 'An incredible aircraft!' exclaimed Robbie
Low afterwards. 'It's absolutely different from what
we've been used to. It's so much faster and smoother,
and feels more natural to do things in. It was just
bloody magic!' John McCrea felt the same. 'I must
admit I was never that keen on the JP. It did everything
reasonably well, but I never came back from a trip
feeling really enthusiastic . . . whereas after forty-five
minutes in the Hawk I got back almost shivering with
enthusiasm. There's none of this delay in the ailerons
that the JP's got. In the JP you moved your hand and
waited, and then it started to turn. This goes *whoop*,
like that, and if you're not careful, it goes *whoop*, right
round. And it goes very, very fast, as well.'

From the start McCrea felt much more optimistic at
Valley than he ever had at Linton. The atmosphere of
the place seemed to suit him better. At Linton he had
been niggled by the insistence on academic precision
that often made flying a chore. At Valley, by contrast,
everything seemed far more relaxed, although still
thoroughly professional. The general feeling that
things were better, coupled with the exciting prospect

of flying the Hawk, helped him through the grind of ground-school.

Another big advantage for him was that, as at OCTU, he got on well with the men immediately in charge of him. Just as Ollie Delaney had helped him greatly at Henlow, so now his primary QFI, Flight Lieutenant John Dobson, and his Squadron Commander, Squadron Leader Dan Walmsley, both took particular trouble to understand him and bring him on.

The discipline at the Valley was easier than any the students had known so far. Although they still addressed the instructors as 'Sir', they had much more freedom of manoeuvre, particularly in the air. 'Our whole aim is to put the onus on *them*,' said Group Captain Blackley. 'The point is that they need an enormous amount of self-discipline. Once a student has taken off solo we have no direct control over what he does, so as soon as they come here they're encouraged to take decisions for themselves. Valley's the first place at which the reins are relaxed.'

One of the first challenges with which the course had to contend was another survival exercise, this time in the mountains of Snowdonia. On the assumption that they had ejected from an aircraft with nothing but their life-jackets and their personal survival packs, they were made to march ten miles into the hills and bivouac in their parachutes for four nights. To supplement their meagre rations they set lines in the streams to catch trout – a pastime at which Bill Harrison proved particularly adept. One highlight of the exercise was the lecture and demonstration on the construction of evasion shelters – a crash course in the art of concealing oneself in enemy territory. The Flight Lieutenant who gave the lecture had a style and delivery all his own, producing hidden men out of an apparently bare hillside like a magician drawing rabbits from a hat.

'OK, then, Gents,' he began. 'Can we have your attention, please? Now, we've got one member of the DS [Directing Staff] literally within ten or fifteen feet of where we're standing. Anyone see him? Fairly obvious? No?

'Give us a shout, Steve. That's not a tin of firewood. Got a guy just crawled in there. Pulled a load of wood on top of him and he's fast asleep. Here – come and look. Most people would say a tin like that, not big enough for a man to hide in. He's not all in it – here's his feet. It's obvious when you get so close. Now that's the sort of place a guy can lie in and quietly kip for hours and hours. He's fairly dry, moderately warm – he's away.

'OK. I've got another evader hidden within fifteen feet of here as well. I'd like you to go and search him out for yourselves. Go get him. See if you can find him . . .

'Anyone know where he is? Are you there, Trevor? You were given the chance to search, Gentlemen. How about our second evader? You'd be amazed how big that little cave is. You didn't even know, did you?'

After dire warnings against giving themselves away by their own smell (far-reaching after several days of living rough) or by injudicious urination, the students were shown a small area of ground and told to choose sites for evasion shelters. Next morning at dawn they would return, conceal themselves, and see if they could survive the three-phase search that would comb the area later.

Back at Valley they began learning the systems of the Hawk in the simulator, which has a full-scale cockpit fitted up so that it tilts in two planes in response to movements of the control column. The instruments, governed by the computer programme, respond realistically to whatever the pilot does, and also to the simulated emergencies fed in as part of the training. The noises incorporated in the programme are exactly those that a pilot would hear in the air. Altogether the ride given by the simulator is sufficiently lifelike to make the equipment a valuable training aid, and the students found they enjoyed working in it, often returning after hours to give themselves extra sessions in the evenings.

As one of the officers in charge of the simulator remarked, 'We can really put someone through it in here. We can move him around the sky, send him out, bring him back, talk him down on radar and give him any emergency to deal with from an engine flame-out to a bird-strike.'

Bird-strike was a serious hazard to anyone flying from Valley. Around the airfield itself a bird-control unit – mounted in a Land-Rover equipped with loud-speakers that broadcast tape-recorded distress cries – kept the sky fairly clear, but at low level anywhere up and down the coast there was always a risk of running into gulls, starlings, pigeons, or one of the rarer species. Most birds just bounced off whatever part of the airframe they hit, but it was essential that a student should react correctly, and instantaneously, if one came through the canopy or went into the engine.

When the real flying started, most of the students learned very fast. They found the Hawk so easy to handle that they were ready to go solo in it after only ten hours or so. Yet the general handling was merely the first phase of the course: the real aim of Valley was to teach them to fly tactically, to train them to get themselves from A to B to C and back, and in general to start using the aeroplane for a purpose.

One tiresome innovation was the wearing of immersion suits, which became mandatory whenever the sea temperature fell below a certain figure. Everyone knew that a pilot *not* wearing an immersion suit would have little or no chance of surviving an ejection into the sea. Even so, it was a chore to have to wear the heavy, thick extra skins, with their tight rubber cuffs and collars. The bulk and heat of the suits made flying still more uncomfortable than it was already, and even sitting around in them was tedious.

It so happened that the weather was exceptionally fine for the first four or five weeks of the flying programme. As a result, each student was able to fly two or three sorties a day, and most of them found that pretty tiring. McCrea, for one, discovered that the Hawk demanded a good deal of mental agility:

'You can get into trouble very quickly, because the Hawk thinks nothing of doing 500 knots. If you leave the throttle in the top left-hand corner and forget it, you're doing 500 knots before you know what's what. I find it happens most coming out of low level, because at 250 feet, 360 knots seems as fast as being in a go-kart, but when you pull up to 2000 feet you seem to be almost stalling, so you automatically put more power on, and then you come back into the circuit and realize you've got 450 knots, which can be a bit embarrassing.'

The further his flying progressed, the more McCrea enjoyed it. After the general handling and instrument phases he went on to formation work and navigation. Soon he realized that what he liked best was low flying, and he described his first solo low-level navigation exercise, which he flew in the middle of June, as the best he had ever done.

The object of this sortie was to fly a large, cross-country circuit, at between 250 and 500 feet, right down through Wales as far as Hereford and Llanelli, and to reach a number of turning-points at the correct times. The route included a wide variety of terrain, from the mountains of north Wales to the undulating farmland of Herefordshire, and the weather was none too good. As McCrea put it, 'There was a lot of cloud around, but it looked as though I could get through the gaps, and I did.'

What pleased him particularly was the tactical element in the exercise. Carried one stage further, the turning-points on the route would become targets over which his aeroplane must arrive at the right moment, so as to co-ordinate his attack with that of others. None of the staff badgered him to make every turn with pedantic precision: as long as he got to the right places

152

at the right times, nobody cared what corners he cut on the way.

Describing the sortie, McCrea said, 'It's hard work – no two ways about it. You shouldn't really look at the scenery, I know. But the scenery goes flashing past. Look-out's the hardest thing, because it's easy to look out and not see. The speed means you've got to look much further ahead than in the JP. Something like a road junction which was useful in a JP is absolutely no good, because it's gone – you know, you just don't *see* road junctions. So you have to use big things like mountains to navigate by.'

For the first time in the whole of his training, McCrea was beginning to emerge from the straitjacket of self-doubt and self-criticism which had hampered him so much. His emergence was accompanied – or perhaps reflected – by the purchase of a new sports car, a £4000, coffee-and-cream TVR, which replaced the yellow Morgan. There had been nothing wrong with the Morgan, he insisted; but the TVR, with its three-litre engine, was still better able to cope with the 200-mile round trip between Valley and his home near Stockport.

While McCrea began to flourish modestly, Robbie Low found his career blighted by a severe stroke of bad luck. He came through ground-school with the rest of his course, went solo in the Hawk, and was just getting his teeth into the flying when he became afflicted by a bunged-up nose and a feeling of fullness in his face, particularly when he bent forward. The station medical officer diagnosed sinusitis, stopped him flying, sent him to bed and prescribed antibiotics and decongestants.

The treatment produced some improvement, but not a complete cure, and the illness dragged on in a puzzling way for weeks. In itself it was nothing serious, but its effect was highly damaging for it meant that Low could not fly, and so fell far behind the rest of the course. As the doctor explained to him, it would be dangerous to fly with sinuses blocked: with the atmospheric pressure decreasing in a climb and then increasing again in a descent, the gas in the sinus passages would first expand and then contract, causing him intense pain and perhaps even injury.

In the end the medical officer began to think that Low might have a form of allergic rhinitis, possibly caused by the stress and anxiety of the flying course, and he sent him south for a consultation with a specialist in the RAF hospital at Wroughton. After a six-hour drive, Low had a five-minute talk with the specialist. He said that antibiotics would never cure the trouble, gave him a different drug and sent him back. The new pills worked immediately, and Low returned to flying – but not before he had lost nearly thirty hours in the air. Whether he would ever catch up was a matter of some doubt, for he had always been a slow learner. Nevertheless, he and the staff made every effort to bring him back into line. He was given priority over all the other members of the course; if several of them were due to fly, it was always he who went first, and he often got in two or three sorties in a day. Everyone felt that he had had particularly bad luck: by common consent he was one of the nicest people on the course, and he seemed to have done nothing to deserve such a setback.

As the course progressed, the students extended their range until they were flying all over Wales, into England and up into the Scottish Highlands. If the weather closed in at Valley after they had taken off, they might sometimes divert to Lossiemouth, on the east coast of Scotland, spend the night there, train in Scotland again the next day, and return to base in the evening.

Their final navigation test, in the middle of July, took the form of a long sortie to the south or to the north, depending on the weather. The sortie to the south went right down to St Mawgan, in Cornwall, and back. The outward leg was flown at high level, at

30,000 feet. Then, off Trevose Point, the student had to let down to low level and come all the way home at 250 feet, via a series of pre-set turning-points. If at any stage things seemed to be going too easily, his instructor in the back seat might suddenly announce: 'Enemy aircraft – four o'clock.' He would be forced into taking violent evasive action and would be driven off track, thus making the job of picking up his route to the next turning-point that much harder. Often, however, the weather created quite enough difficulties anyway, and students trying to fly their low-level route would find themselves confronted by low clouds sitting on the hills ahead of them. Their reactions then earned them good or bad marks from the instructor.

'Sometimes they see some weather sat on a hill,' said Squadron Leader Walmsley, 'and if it's on track they fly straight towards it. They sit there and sit there and sit there. I just wait for the decision, and sometimes it never comes. In the end they say, "What do you want me to do, sir?" "Oh – just go ahead and crash."

'I leave it as late as I can, and then take control, and go round the weather and give them a black mark, because obviously you can't do things like that. There's a lot of hillsides spattered with pilots.

'Some students tend to *over* map-read. They go thumbing along a straight line, getting it all right, but then their speed starts to go wrong, or the heading goes wrong, and suddenly they find that things on the ground aren't matching up with what they've got on the map. At that moment they're inclined to panic. They divert still further from the heading and go slower, and it all gets worse and worse. Eventually they're not with it at all.

'What it means is that they aren't flying the way they've been taught. They aren't looking out enough. Look-out's not a natural function. You've got to practise it.'

Discussing this final navigation test, John McCrea saw it as a simulation of a real raid on an enemy country. The first part, he said, represented the outward transit over England, flown as high as possible to save fuel. 'Then you'd let down to a point on the coast of Europe and fly across any country that was between you and the enemy, which I suppose is Russia. You'd have to fly very accurately, because there'd be no navigational aids whatever, and there *would* be missile sites that we'd have marked on our maps. The aim would be to hit a target and turn around and come out as fast and low as possible, because once you'd hit the target they'd obviously know you were about and they'd be looking for you. So you'd have to choose a route which you'd hope they wouldn't guess, but one that would get you out with sufficient fuel to reach home.'

McCrea duly passed the test on 11 July, and if he did not fly as accurately as he might have, at least he completed the course. His debrief with Squadron Leader Walmsley, who tested him, gave a good idea of the easy *rapport* that had developed between instructor and pupil.

WALMSLEY: Coming up here, you sort of let it happen. You didn't go for any heading – you just wallowed around a bit. You'd hacked it by then. The rain had gone. The will to live, desire to get home – all the rest of it.

McCREA: I knew I'd see Valley after a while.

WALMSLEY: I know. I thought you were using the Francis Chichester ten per cent error – 'We'll hit the coast and hope.' There's the heading. Fly it. OK? General points. You're too low at times. Definitely. I like low flying, but, by God, sometimes those trees were looking in the cockpit.

McCREA: All right, sir. I'm sorry.

WALMSLEY: And some of the sheep didn't like it much, either. So don't skim ridges. Use the aeroplane, make it do what you want it to do, but don't just go on a mean line *bonk* over one ridge, and *bonk* over the valley. You know, fly across the valley, but don't miss that ridge by fifty feet, as you were doing at times.

McCREA: All right, sir.

WALMSLEY: More fuel checks. They were coming, but not very many. We got one about there, somewhere . . .

McCREA: We got one at Five, definitely.

WALMSLEY: We got one at Five, did we? OK. And then we didn't get one for . . .

McCREA: We got one about Eleven.

WALMSLEY: It was a massive one, then. Shout it. Convince me you're giving it. OK? Do watch that low flying, though. Going back to this point . . . coming along here, I was thinking you could save yourself a minute – and in the end you thought it too. It was a big, enormous mental process, and I could hear the wheels grinding, but that was a good start. So we saved a minute by cutting that corner.

One characteristic McCrea liked in Walmsley was his habit of saying what he meant in plain terms. Discussing what sort of man the RAF needed as a pilot, for instance, he gave a forthright outline: 'He's got to fit the bill, and in fast-jet flying it's easy to see why. You're not going to go to war with a wanker on your wing who you can't trust or even like. You know – you'd probably get ten miles down the road and lose him. So you've got to be a unit, and you've got to be all similar types.

'We are all similar types – balanced extroverts, somebody called us. We're all that, and it's quite logical. If you go to war in a four-ship or a six-ship, you've got to like the next guy, and you've got to trust the leader. You've got to know what he's going to do, and he's got to think like you do. So it's logical – yes. Balanced extroverts. What does that mean? Well – it's the way of life we lead. Socially we tend to stick together. We have the mess, and we all drink beer to excess on Friday evenings. That sort of thing.'

After his good start at Valley, McCrea for some reason hit a sticky patch in the middle of the course. The reason was never clear either to himself or to his instructors. But as he struggled through it he realized more and more clearly that his real bent was for low flying, and in due course he changed his first choice of aircraft from Phantom to Buccaneer, the specialist low-level fighter-bomber. Not that it was up to the staff at Valley to recommend the students for posting to particular types: they merely decided whether a student was fit to continue in the fast-jet stream and go on to the Tactical Weapons Unit at Brawdy, or whether he should be diverted to some slower form of flying.

In spite of the efforts made on his behalf by himself and others, Robbie Low never did catch up. He was bottom of the course on every count, and for some time before the end it was clear to the instructors that he was not going to measure up to the demands of the TWU. Nevertheless they kept him going and got him through the Valley syllabus.

The climax of the flying programme was the final handling test, in which all the elements the students had learned came together. A typical sortie would include a high-level transit, a let-down over southern England, an away-landing at another airfield, a simulated emergency, a diversion to another airfield again, a roller there, a low-level run to attack a target at the precise time laid down before take-off, a return to Anglesey, a few circuits at Mona (Valley's relief airfield) and back to base. All this, except any emergencies the instructor might call, had to be planned by the student himself.

As late as his last run-up sortie before the test, Low was still capable of making a serious and potentially dangerous mistake. He flew most of the route outlined above successfully, but when told to divert to Wittering because of a simulated fuel shortage, he went straight into the circuit without calling up air-traffic control. The first radio call he made to the tower was 'Finals –

three greens' requesting immediate permission to land. Although the tower gave him permission, the whole incident was, as his instructor put it afterwards, 'rather embarrassing, because it could have screwed up a lot of people. You can't just go into an airway without being positively under someone's radar control. There could have been several aircraft in the circuit that we didn't know about – and any there were didn't know about us.'

In spite of several errors, Low passed his FHT at the beginning of September, as did McCrea, and both won their wings. But whereas McCrea, after his bad patch, had continued to improve steadily, and was recommended for the TWU, Low was not considered strong enough for either a single-seat or even a twin-seat high-performance role. He was therefore recommended for Canberras.

The Wings ceremony was held in the officers' mess on 12 September 1980. Though not accompanied by a church service or a parade, it was nonetheless a highly charged occasion, marking as it did the culmination of so much effort and elevation to a new status. Many relatives and friends came to the ceremony, which represented – in the words of Flight Lieutenant John Dobson – 'a very personal milestone' in the careers of the participants.

'These pilots,' he said, 'have shown that they are man enough to meet the tremendous demands of flying modern combat aircraft . . . Defence, of course, is an emotive issue, but of one thing I'm sure, and that is that if we in this country, and indeed in NATO, don't show that we have the will and the ability to defend ourselves, then any potential aggressor may think we're an easy prey.

'The great majority of us value the freedoms that we have in the west, and those freedoms have got to be defended. That's why I'm particularly pleased that these young pilots have chosen the defensive, determined role that they will play in the Royal Air Force during the years ahead.'

The wings themselves were laid out on a silver tray, and after the Chaplain had blessed them, Squadron Leader Walmsley gave quick verbal portraits of all the members of the course. The Review Officer, Air Vice Marshal John Sutton, then presented the wings, lodging one pair on the velcro strip already in position on each graduand's uniform. In his speech he looked briefly ahead to their careers. 'I think I can safely say that in terms of challenge and achievement, military flying is second to none,' he told them. 'And the nearer to the front line you get, the more exhilarating it becomes.'

10

Learning to Kill

The Tactical Weapons Unit at Brawdy is the place at which flying training ceases to be a game. So far the students have learned how to handle aircraft; but now they are taught how to use them for a lethal purpose – how to direct and position them as weapon-platforms, for the delivery of rockets, bombs and cannon-fire. In other words, they are taught to kill.

When John McCrea's course reached Brawdy in October 1980, the concept was put straight to them on the first day by the commander of 234 Squadron, Squadron Leader Mike Johnson. They were there to be trained as professional killers, he told them: from now on they must think in those terms and accept the responsibility. They must be prepared to fight for what they believed in, and stand committed to the cause of the country's freedom.

The initial response was flippant, but Squadron Leader Johnson had seen that sort of reaction before and he knew that it concealed a deep unease. He also knew that over the next sixteen weeks every student would, in his own particular fashion, come to terms with the fact that he had entered a new and ruthless environment.

The courses at Brawdy are very small: only six or seven students on each. Two different courses, one eight weeks ahead of the other, run together, so that the total population of students on 234 Squadron at any one time is about fourteen. Since there are a dozen instructors, the levels of tuition and supervision are extremely high.

Here, for the first time, students and instructors share the same crew-room, instead of being accommodated separately. Students no longer address instructors as 'Sir', but call them by their Christian names. Discipline is so relaxed as to appear non-existent. Certainly it is quite informal. As one of the instructors put it, 'We don't need the old form of military discipline such as you get in the Army or Navy, because we're so much more technical. Everyone realizes that we're dealing with machines that could kill us in seconds.' And yet, on the ground no less than in the air, a form of discipline exists. The far greater experience of the instructors, all of whom are fast-jet pilots in their own right, gives them a natural authority which they can exert if they need to. Instructor-student relationships, though close, are not quite so matey as the Christian-name terms might make them appear.

All who work there agree that Brawdy is a godforsaken place. The airfield is just inland from the cliffs of what is now officially know as Dyfed, but what everyone still calls and thinks of as Pembrokeshire. In summer the roads are choked with the cars and caravans of holidaymakers, but in winter the whole area goes dead. The weather is notoriously bad, and it is common for the airfield to be closed for days on end by the dreaded 'Brawdy clamp' – a form of sea fog or low cloud which, when it has settled, is maddeningly slow to clear.

In terms of entertainment, the area is at the back of beyond. There is nothing in the neighbourhood except the cinema in Haverfordwest, ten miles away, and a few country pubs, which are pinpointed on a map in the crew-room, with sharp comments on merits and shortcomings.

On the station itself, the amenities are only a little better. Because the officers' mess began life as a naval wardroom (Brawdy having been originally a naval

162

airfield) it is of a definitely non-RAF design, and even more gloomy than messes laid out on normal Air Force lines. Indeed, John McCrea and his friends found it *so* dismal that four of them decided to rent a house in the neighbouring village of Solva and live there instead.

Yet nobody in the RAF is posted to Brawdy for a holiday or to enjoy the surroundings; tactical flying and weapon training are the twin *raisons d'être* of the station, and as soon as a new course arrives, both begin at once.

At least the students do not have to learn to fly new aeroplanes. The Hawks at Brawdy are the same as those at Valley, except that they are fitted to carry and fire live weapons, and are painted camouflage green and grey instead of red and white – a colour scheme which, intentionally, makes them hard to see at low level. The camouflage had a marked effect on the students: flying these warlike aircraft seemed an altogether more serious business, requiring greater commitment, than flying the red-and-white toys at Valley.

There was plenty else to learn, the first element of the syllabus being tactical formation-flying. The importance of maintaining good formation at low level can hardly be overstressed, for in it lies the pilot's main protection from attack by enemy aircraft. Since a pilot cannot see straight behind him, somebody else must watch his six o'clock. Hence the concept of standard defensive battle formation, in which two aircraft, or two pairs of aircraft, keep station some 1500 to 2000 yards apart, each watching the other's six. To the civilian this may sound merely like one more sensible precaution, but in the air it is a matter of life and death. As one of the instructors at Brawdy put it: 'You can be superbly on track, everything just right, but have your arse shot off because of poor formation. If he sees you and you don't see him, you're going to die.'

The responsibility of leading a tactical formation immediately sets a student a new psychological problem. No longer is he merely involved with his own cockpit. He has to think on a far bigger scale, to project himself out into space and imagine how he can manoeuvre an entity over a mile wide. Soon this becomes a basic skill, like riding a bicycle or walking along a pavement without bumping into people: once he knows how to do it, he does it automatically. But before he gains confidence, it can be extremely harassing.

Simultaneously, a start is made on air gunnery, beginning with an exercise called Cine-weave, a form of tail-chase in which the pilot starts learning how to keep his gunsight trained on the aeroplane ahead of him. The target aircraft flies a precise pattern, starting off in a 45-degree banked turn at 400 knots. As soon as the second pilot calls 'Com-*mence!*' over the radio, the leader hits his stop-watch button. Three seconds later he increases the turn to a four-g break to the left. At twelve seconds he reduces the angle of bank to 30 degrees and starts a barrel roll.

The aim of the attacking pilot is to stabilize at 300 yards behind the leader. In real life he would go as close as he could, to make sure of the kill; but for exercise purposes the limit is set at 200 yards, and if he goes closer than that he forfeits all the points which he scores for keeping in range. He also scores points if he holds the pipper of his gunsight steady on the back of the enemy's cockpit. In a typical sortie the student should get in about seven consecutive attacks, and he films the five best by depressing a button on the control column to operate the gunsight camera. The films are developed within a few minutes of his landing, and analysed during the debrief.

The next subjects to be covered are the arts of strafing, rocketing, and bombing, with live weapons, on the range at Pembrey, a deserted airfield just down the coast from Brawdy. Now for the first time, the nature of the student's killer status begins to come home to him. As he sees rockets scorch fierily away from under his wings, or watches his bombs blast up the mud and water round the target, he realizes that he is an agent of death and destruction. The message comes over even more clearly in discussions on air-combat: the prime target is the 'soft part' of the enemy aircraft – in other words, the pilot. The target is another human being.

Most students avoid the moral questions involved by sheltering behind the fact that their aeroplanes distance them from the enemy. It is not like hand-to-hand fighting, they say: the aeroplane makes every-thing more impersonal. Besides, you are so busy flying the thing, trying to avoid being shot down and con-centrating on all your various weapon switches, that you scarcely have time to think what you are doing to the enemy.

Whatever their deeper feelings, all the students enjoy the range sorties. Moreover, competition between them is fostered deliberately. The score for every bomb they drop, for every rocket or bullet they fire, is put up on a board in the corridor of the squadron's administrative block, where all passers-by can see it. The scores themselves are not particularly important: what does matter is that their public display keeps everybody sharp.

In the middle of the course, one of John McCrea's colleagues, Howard Davies, thought he had devised a new method of bomb-aiming. A university graduate with a degree in engineering, Davies studied the manuals, thought he might do better by aiming and launching his bombs in a slightly different fashion, and tried his patent method – at first with some success, but not with any lasting improvement.

The next new element is tactical formation-flying while navigating at low level. Again, this is an exten-sion of the low-level work the students have done at Valley, but all the same it is a formidable step forward. At first one student leads another aeroplane in a simple formation, with an instructor in the chase aircraft, as at Valley; but then the formation is changed to the tactical one he learned earlier, and here his problems begin. Down at 250 feet, with the Welsh hills rising above him on all sides, he finds it an enormous strain to control and manoeuvre a formation over a mile wide.

Brawdy is particularly well placed for low-level exercises. The mountains of central and north Wales lie in easy reach to the north, and in the opposite direction the wilds of Devon and Cornwall are almost equally accessible. In fact, after a recent fundamental rewriting of the rules, the whole of England, Wales, and Scotland have become one huge low-flying area, only cities, towns, industrial complexes, hospitals and other sensitive areas being out of bounds, so that it is now possible to fly low more or less anywhere. Even so, it is obviously desirable to stick as far as possible to the areas least-inhabited.

Complaints from the public hardly impinge on the students, for most of them are fielded at higher level. Yet everyone is keenly aware that low flying is an irritation to humans and a menace to livestock, sheep and horses particularly. What is needed, in the view of Mike Johnson, is a far more vigorous public-relations campaign by the RAF to put across the point of the exercise.

'Low flying needs much more explanation,' he says. 'What we have to put over is the fact that if hostilities broke out in Europe, the area below 250 feet is the only one in which we could hope to survive. If we went higher than that, we could expect to be knocked down pretty quickly. If you're going to have a realistic capability, you must have realistic training – and low flying is one of those things at which you've got to have constant practice. Unless you train all the time, you become a danger to yourself and everybody else.'

Hence the emphasis at Brawdy on low-level work. For a pilot travelling seven miles a minute at 250 feet, one obvious essential is good navigation: he must be able to find his way to a target and back. The compass fitted in the RAF Hawks is notoriously unreliable, and liable to topple after hard manoeuvring; but in any case, down in the valleys at low level a compass is of only limited use. Much depends on a pilot's skill at reading his maps and correlating the features marked on them with those he sees on the ground.

In planning their sorties, pilots soon develop a specialized map-reading skill. What they are looking for are features that will stand out from the air and help them first to follow a particular route and then guide them in to the target. Spot-heights are obviously good in this respect; so are television and radio masts, which are usually on high ground. Woods can be good, provided they are isolated, but lakes are not so good on the whole for, although on the map they look beautifully conspicuous, marked blue, on the ground they are always in hollows and therefore may be difficult to see until the last moment, and too late. Funnel-features – two ridges converging, or a road and railway coming together – are particularly prized.

There is a subtle difference between the map-reading of a pilot and that of a motorist. It does not matter to the pilot what country it is below him: the signposts, and the language the people speak, are immaterial to him. He cannot stop to read a sign or ask the way or verify what particular village or town it is that he has reached. His only way of checking is by reference to what he can see from above. Thus a pilot flying over Wales might just as well be over France or Germany or (God forbid) Russia: provided he reads his map properly, he will find his way to the target and back.

The normal problems of navigation are soon augmented by the introduction of evasion exercises. A student on track from A to B is 'bounced' by an instructor who makes a mock attack, aiming to drive him off course. The student must counter the attack – either by turning straight towards the bounce, so that he passes head-on and harmlessly in the opposite direction, or by manoeuvring away from him – and

167

then, as soon as possible, get back on his original heading. (Two aircraft, passing on opposite courses, are out of sight of each other in a few seconds.) At low level students are not allowed to pull more than four g in evasion manoeuvres; even so, as one instructor put it, 'when you're down below 500 feet and doing 420 knots, with high ground all round you and an aircraft coming down on you from above so that you're looking over your shoulder all the time, that's quite enough'.

Altogether, the students find the flying a great deal more violent than any they have done before; and no activity is more violent than air-combat, in which they often pull eight g briefly and sustain seven g for considerable periods. (The Hawk is so strongly built that it can be stressed to ten g without any special checks having to be made afterwards – more than any other aeroplane in RAF service. The normal limit on a Phantom, for comparison, is six g, and if a pilot pulls more than that the aircraft has to be inspected before it can be certified safe.)

The sheer physical strain of air-combat is not easily appreciated by someone who has never known it. The students come down from a half-hour session soaked through with sweat and often so exhausted that it would be dangerous for them to fly another sortie that day. They also find at first that the continuous high-g manoeuvring plays havoc with semi-circular canals in their ears. They may feel all right until they have landed and taxied back to the line, but as soon as they stop and put their heads down to replace the ejector seat safety-pin, they find everything spinning round.

The first time that John McCrea came to rest after an air-combat sortie, he thought he felt the whole aeroplane jump into the air. Then he got the impression that it was rolling backwards, so he hastily checked the handbrake. When he climbed out of the aircraft he had difficulty standing up, and the giddiness took three-quarters of an hour to wear off.

The instructors, whose tour of duty lasts three years,

find that the muscles in their necks grow so much from the effort of supporting their heads that they need a bigger size in shirts (the effect of pulling eight g is to make one's head weight about fifty pounds). They also tend to fall victim to an ailment known as 'Hawk neck' – muscles strained partly by the effort of combating g, and partly by the need to maintain a look-out upwards and backwards through the Hawk's large canopy.

In spite of the stress, many students find air-combat the most enjoyable part of the whole syllabus. Yet it is less easy than they imagine before they start. 'They think they know all about it,' said Flt Lt Bob Burrough, second-in-command of 234 Squadron when John McCrea went through. 'Everyone's familiar with Battle of Britain-type dogfights. They think they've seen it all – but it's very different from what they expect.'

The air-combat training is done at high level – 10,000 feet or more. It starts with an extension of the tail-chasing done at Linton and Valley, one aeroplane following another, trying to keep with it. But this is just one facet of air-combat, and in fact the final phase: the object of the whole exercise is to position one's aircraft between 300 and 500 yards behind the bogie and to hold the pipper of the gunsight steady on the cockpit for half a second. Most modern aeroplanes will survive hits in the wing, but the cockpit is the vulnerable heart: track that for half a second, or the rest of the airframe for two seconds, and you will have a kill. The problem is to come anywhere near that lethal position. At first students often find they are stuck in a level, turning fight, pulling round as hard as they can but unable to turn any harder than the enemy. They end up in a stalemate because they lack the experience to break the pattern.

For the first two sorties they are accompanied by an instructor in the back seat, who shows them a few basic manoeuvres. Then the instructors become the enemy and fly against them in one-v-one combats. The theoretical aim in all these is to go for the collision point – to fly straight for the bogie, which though not quite as dangerous as it sounds is nevertheless not a particularly safe pastime. With two aeroplanes converging at a combined speed of over 800 knots there is not much time to recover from a mistake.

In the words of Bob Burrough, 'Combat is a bit like dancing. There's a certain sequence of events that you must follow, but you can always slip in a series of manoeuvres to assist yourself. Most combats are lost rather than won: you're always turning to stop yourself being killed, but at the same time waiting for the other guy to make a mistake. Is he going to put himself on a predictable trajectory? Has he got his aircraft pointing too high, and lost too much speed? Is he going to be unable to manoeuvre as fast as I can? If he goes predictable, I may be able to fly my aeroplane to the collision point without him being able to do anything about it.'

In a specially-compiled handbook, a student can read how to execute a whole series of manoeuvres, including a high-speed yo-yo – a kind of wing-over. But only by actually trying them out does he find what will and will not work. Only through practice does he learn how to use the vertical dimension to best advantage, and only through practice does he discover the value of bluff – of pretending to be at a disadvantage and luring the bogie into what he thinks will be a good position for himself. Because of their far greater experience, the instructors could outfly the students completely if they tried to. They therefore tailor their flying to push the learners as hard as they think wise – and push them they do, into positions which, if not positively dangerous, are very nearly that. Thus considerable mental strain is added to the physical stress of a sortie. Every day brings a new struggle.

A two-v-one – in which a pair of aeroplanes attack one bogie – can be even more demanding. In theory it should be relatively simple for two aircraft to deal with one; but in practice the difficulties are formidable. One of the tactics taught is 'free and engaged': while the first aircraft tries to punch the bogie on the nose, the other goes round behind him, at a distance, aiming to run in unseen and make a quick kill while his attention is engaged elsewhere.

The theory is easier than its execution: to the free aeroplane, three miles off, the two locked in combat are merely whirling specks. In choosing his moment of re-entry, the free pilot must somehow decide where the bogie will be by the time he is back within reach. If, when he makes his dash, the bogie is coming towards him, the combined closing speed will be over 800 knots, so that he will have less than twenty seconds in which to call his partner on the radio and explain his plan of attack.

The position then *is* potentially dangerous. The free aeroplane may come up and engage the bogie beneath the aircraft already fighting him. In Bob Burrough's words, 'Everything starts happening belly-up, and students do find it a bit confusing. It's a tough environment altogether.'

John McCrea, in his first solo air-combat, thought for a few glorious moments that he had got Bob Burrough cold. As usual the pair set off in defensive battle formation, some 1500 yards apart, and then separated, both heading outwards. As soon as Burrough felt sure McCrea could no longer see him, he called for both of them to turn in and start the hunt.

'I think I fooled him by mistake,' McCrea said afterwards. 'It was like a beginner playing chess against a grand master. There are the standard opening moves, but if you do something ridiculous it may take him a few moves to recover. Somehow I managed to get him unsighted, and there he was, climbing up in front of me. I thought, I'm going to get him, but when I rolled upside down the VHF radio suddenly dropped out of its socket, so that I couldn't reach it to change frequencies. That meant I had to pack it in, so I waggled my wings to say 'terminate' and went home.'

McCrea turned out not to enjoy air-combat as much as some of his colleagues. He preferred to be at low level, and said so in his typically robust northern fashion: 'I'm all right as long as I'm in sight of the ground, but up there, it's a bugger.' Nevertheless, he became quite proficient at high level, not least because he was prepared to fly to his own physical limits.

'I find that at anything above seven g I start to grey out,' he reported. 'But I just keep bloody pulling and hope for the best. I don't ever go unconscious. What happens first is that I get tunnel vision: all I can see is two white circles, framed by the canopy. Then if I pull more than that the picture goes completely, and it's like being in a dark cloud.

'I can still think and talk. So if I'm in a turn, and know I'm not going to hit the ground or the other bloke, there's no reason why I shouldn't keep pulling. The second I relax, sight comes back.'

A thirty-minute tape recording, taken from McCrea's intercom during an air-combat sortie, was found to consist of eighty per cent of groans, fifteen per cent of imprecations (mostly obscene), and only five per cent of useful exchanges with his opponent.

Like most of his mates, McCrea found the first few weeks of the course a struggle, and not until the second half, when everything was more familiar, did he really begin to enjoy it. 'He's actually smiling now,' said one of the instructors, later on. 'But it was a dreadful job to get a smile out of him at first. Most students try to drag compliments out of the staff, but John's the opposite. If he comes back from the range having dropped three good bombs and one bad one, he'll say he deserved the bad one.'

Gradually, as his confidence increased, McCrea began finally to shed his habit of self-disparagement. He owed much to Bob Burrough, who recognized in him the very problems that he himself had been through in training, and talked him through them. Yet he was by no means the only one who felt the strain.

172

Even Paul Field, able pilot though he was, had to be persuaded to keep going by careful staff counselling; Louis McQuade, for all his aggression, also nearly went under.

Everyone found that the exhaustion engendered by the flying programme tended to damp down social activity in the evenings. 'After you've flown a couple of combat sorties,' said one student, 'your eyeballs and eyesockets are aching horribly, and your neck feels as if it had had a going over from a KGB masseur. So all you really want to do is go to bed.'

Nevertheless, the course-members did sometimes rouse themselves sufficiently to go out for a few beers in one of the local pubs, and they established a regular habit of sallying forth on Wednesday evenings for a curry supper at the Druidstone, an inn down on the coast whose landlord had been out east and had absorbed a few Indian culinary secrets. The heat of his chicken vindaloo, together with its accompanying lime pickle, made it *necessary*, rather than just pleasant, to order several more pints.

For McCrea and his colleagues, Brawdy was essentially a winter place. The long, dark, wet evenings did not encourage exploration of the surrounding countryside or coast; rather, the students tended to stay at home, or at most to make the short trek to the Royal George, the cosy pub in Solva.

The best place to observe a course of students is in the communal crew-room on the first floor of the squadron building. The room is comfortable, if a bit shabby. Armless easy chairs line two sides of it. In one corner there are a couple of tables, on which somebody is generally working at a map, and in the opposite one the bar for making tea, coffee, and snacks. Always, it seems, someone is brewing something or slapping together great thick sandwiches from sliced bread and lumps of cheddar hacked off a seven-pound bar. Peanut butter and cheese spread are other standbys. On working days nobody goes back to the mess for lunch: either they survive unhealthily on sandwiches, or else they go out to a tiny aircrew buffet a few yards from the hangar, where a limited range of hot food is available.

Almost everything in the crew-room is to do with flying. The pictures – colour photographs and reproductions of paintings – are all of aeroplanes. There is a large black silhouette of an aircraft painted on the centre of the ceiling. Over the telephone hang the celebrated Supersonic Knickers (brilliant turquoise and gold) with their accompanying legend: 'This trophy was captured, live, from "The Exotic Eva" at the Gribble Inn, Torrington, on 4 May 1973 by Officers of 234 Squadron. Flown at a speed in excess of M.1.0 on May 10.'

In the crew-room the atmosphere is apparently relaxed. Everyone wears flying gear of one kind or another. Most people are in their heavy immersion suits, unzipped for ventilation. There is constant coming and going. In bad weather, when flying is impossible, a broody silence is inclined to fall; but on good days, when the scream of aeroplanes taking off and landing outside the windows constantly drowns out the conversation, the chatter is brisk and bawdy.

Behind the superficial frivolity, however, there is considerable tension. It becomes manifest in the way one student keeps whistling the theme from the first movement of Beethoven's Emperor Concerto: he whistles quite accurately, but far louder than is comfortable, and so insistently that someone else suddenly yells at him to lay off. Abrupt outbreaks of shouted banter confirm that nerves are on edge.

No one here is afraid of flying: if they were, they would never have got as far as Brawdy. Rather, they are nervous of doing poorly in their next sortie, of making mistakes, of not being able to cope, of letting themselves down. For the past two years, every day's flying has been an examination in itself. Failure to

174

complete the programme of a sortie means falling behind. To please the instructors here is no use: the students are fighting against themselves, and they know when they succeed or fail.

Their attitude towards danger is complex and – to a civilian – slightly baffling. 'We're not doing anything dangerous,' says one pilot after another, instructors as well as students. All maintain that their work is perfectly safe. Pressed a little, they will admit that it is possible to think of occupations less hazardous than flying jets up the Welsh valleys at seven miles a minute; but what they really mean is that they do not take unnecessary risks. This is undoubtedly true: their planning and execution alike are extremely thorough and careful. All the same, they know perfectly well that their profession is inherently hazardous.

To prove it, the crew-room at Brawdy is littered with the official accident reports put out by the Ministry of Defence after every crash or serious incident. Students and instructors study them constantly, pouncing on any new one that comes in as if it were a fresh copy of *Playboy*. Their fascination is not exactly morbid – more technical. By studying minutely what went wrong with someone else's aeroplane, and how the crew reacted to the emergency, they are gleaning information that may one day stand them in good stead and perhaps even save their lives. Even the fatal accidents are freely discussed: the more pilot errors or mechanical failures are talked about, the better chance the survivors have of avoiding any repetition. And in talking about death there is no embarrassment or hushed reverence: pilots reminisce about good friends who have been killed in the most matter-of-fact way.

Accidents apart, the talk is about flying, flying and still more flying. Girls and cars sometimes struggle into the conversation for a few minutes, but always it comes back to the central subject. This is one positive merit of the shared crew-room: the students learn a great deal merely from listening to the instructors'

175

stories. Even a tale told for entertainment packs educational punch. If anyone wants a first-hand account of what it is like to bang out of a Phantom, for instance, he can get one from Flt Lt Kevin Toal, who had to eject at ground level in Germany when the aeroplane of which he was navigator attempted to take off without its folding wings locked down. He suffered a broken ankle and compression fractures of the spine, but after a spell in hospital recovered fully and returned to active service.

It is hard to describe the atmosphere on the squadron without making it sound drab, which it is not. It is certainly not intellectual; nobody seems to read non-technical books much, or to talk about them, or music or the theatre. It is not flamboyant or swashbuckling – nobody swaggers about saying 'Whacko!' except perhaps in self-parody. What it is, perhaps, is *professional*: everybody is not only working hard, but also intensely interested in the job being done, absorbed in their chosen existence. In a way the people are like bees in a hive: they spend their whole time pressing on with the job, which happens to be their life as well.

The enthusiasm for getting airborne is unlimited. 'Anyone want to come in the back seat of my Meteor?' an instructor calls into the crew-room. 'Yes!' yell three or four people. One is chosen and goes off in a storm of repartee. 'Hope you're bloody well insured,' someone shouts. 'No ejection seat in the back of that thing, you know.' Back seats are often available in instructors' aircraft, and almost always they are filled.

The pressure on the students is carefully orchestrated by the instructing staff, whose aim is to push each man as hard as is good for him. At weekly meetings, progress and character are carefully analysed. Most students change considerably during their four months at Brawdy, maturing as leaders and people besides acquiring new skills as pilots. By fine tuning of the programme the instructors can generally nudge every

176

individual in the right direction. As Mike Johnson put it, 'The whole question is, what does a person do when the pressure builds up? How does he order his priorities?

'Sometimes on a low-level sortie we see a student progressing on track, all OK, and then suddenly, without saying anything, he climbs, slows down, and disappears into the middle distance. We know just what's happened: his mind has suddenly dumped – gone blank. It's as if he's reading a book, and his eyes are still following the lines, but his mind's gone somewhere else. When we see that happen, we probably let him go for a minute or two, and then nudge him back to reality.'

The pressure is likely to be greatest of all during the SAPs, or simulated attack profiles, in which students are required to fly low-level sorties against real targets in Wales or Devon. At first with a good deal of help, but at the end on their own, they are given a couple of targets – the pump-house on a dam, a bridge, or an isolated group of buildings – and told to plan an entire mission against it. They must work out a tactical route to and from the targets, plan their fuel for the fifty-minute sortie, choose from the map features which will help them navigate and acquire the targets, and set rendezvous at which they can rejoin formation if they are driven off-track by a bounce. Always the emphasis is on thorough preparation: students must learn the absolute necessity of packing away in their minds the information they will need later, so that when they come to fly they have all the knowledge they need immediately to hand and can devote ninety-five per cent of their attention to the business of navigating, keeping formation and maintaining a lookout for bogies.

Always, at the briefing that precedes a sortie, a lighthearted scenario is set: the revolting Devonians are attacking in conjunction with the Viet Taff, for instance, and the strike on the dam power-house is essential to deny the Nationalists their water for beer-making. Yet, if the background is deliberately ridiculous, the sortie itself is highly professional, and not far from the real thing.

One of the authors, Duff Hart-Davis, was lucky enough to join two students and their instructors flying SAP No 4, halfway through the SAP programme. The four-ship mission was commanded by Flt Lt Wyn Evans, a former Jaguar pilot, who also led one of the pairs; the other pair was led by Squadron Leader Johnson, a Lightning pilot and air-weapons specialist. The two students, Steve and Gerry, were to act as wing-men, following the leaders.

At the briefing Flt Lt Evans handed round photographs of the targets, the first a set of buildings in a wood, and the second an electronics site. 'Here's our IP for the first,' he said. 'Our run-in's on heading 143. Typical Devon countryside – most confusing. Between twenty-five and thirty seconds we'll get that main road and the power cables. At forty seconds I should acquire this road running parallel to my track. That tiny village just on my left is the pull-up point.

'When I can see the target I'll call "In visual", and I want everyone else to do the same. For you, "In visual" means "I can see the target and the aeroplane in front of me." If you can't fulfil either of those conditions, call "No contact" and *stay high* . . .'

For the second target there was an extra hazard – the height of the mast above the electronics site. 'I want you to have the pipper buried in the main building,' Flt Lt Evans told the students. 'But be aware of the fact that the mast is *above your flight line* – so I don't want anybody closer than 900 yards. When you feel you're close enough, take your finger off the button and recover. I'll give marks for people playing chicken, but I won't give marks for people pressing too close . . .'

After take-off we climbed straight out over the sea and then, by means of two port-nineties, turned up

178

the coast and back inland, to come in over the cliffs at 1000 feet and so avoid the gulls, which have a dangerous habit of hang-gliding above the shore. Thereafter we let down to our tactical height.

From 250 feet, the sodden Welsh hill farms appeared to unreel as though carried by a giant conveyor belt. In country as undulating as this it is impossible to maintain 250 feet above the ground precisely; so at one moment we were deep in a valley, with the slopes above us on either side, and at the next we were skirting the brown, bare shoulders of a hill like a grouse following the contours.

A remark made by one of the pilots in the crew-room came back into my head. 'The Hawk's a buoyant, vibrant little aeroplane,' he said. Now I saw what he meant. Buoyant, yes: it bounced around all over the place. The ride was like that of a racing car going at 100 mph on rock-hard tyres and suspension. Vibrant, yes: it was alive with twitch and flutter.

'Number Four's hanging on well,' said Mike Johnson approvingly. By twisting my head round, I could just see him lifting and falling a couple of hundred yards behind our right wing-tip. Whatever we did, he did also. Every now and then our other pair disappeared down a friendly valley that ran parallel to our course, then skimmed into view again as they lifted to clear a ridge.

A quick transit over the Bristol Channel brought us to Devon, greener and neater than Wales, but also more anonymous, with fewer distinctive features. As we began the run-in for the first target, I thought I was going to be able to follow our progress easily on the large-scale map – but not at all.

Everything started happening far too fast. We were right down low and travelling at 285 yards per second. We were also buffeting and twisting. The landscape beneath us came heaving and barrelling past so quickly that it was useless to spend time pondering about whether the wood or hill or crossroads one could see ahead corresponded with one marked on the map. The only thing to do was to look quickly, make an instant decision and look ahead again. I wondered wildly how anyone – student or instructor – could fly this low and fast and map-read simultaneously.

'There's the main road,' Mike suddenly announced, 'and the powerlines. IP coming up.'

Out of the air came the single word, 'Switches!' I hit the button of my stop-watch and saw the hand start round the dial. But the fact that the clock was going seemed to accelerate the passage of time still further. Fields, hedges, lanes whizzed past underneath. Before I picked up any more landmarks, thirty seconds had gone and we were almost at the pull-up point. At forty-seven seconds we banked hard to the left, to come into line behind the lead pair. Then we banked to the right. The landscape wheeled so crazily that I never saw the village marking the actual pull-up point. Only through a haze did I realize that we were climbing, levelling out, tipping in.

Then we were definitely going down the dive. There were woods ahead, as there should be. But where the hell was the target in its clearing? I picked up *a* clearing, slightly off the nose to our right. I scanned it in vain for buildings. At the last second I looked straight ahead and realized that the target was dead on the nose. The bright ring of the gunsight was framing the complex of buildings, the dot of the pipper steady on its centre. The group grew bigger until the main building alone filled the ring of the sight, but only for an instant: with a sickening six-g heave we pulled out of the dive and flashed above it. With quick calls of 'Out contact' the other pilots reported that they had completed their attacks. The formation regrouped and headed due south.

Now Dartmoor was on our left. Its bleak humps, still brown and winter-dead, were well above us. In three minutes we slipped down into the valley of the Tamar. One port-ninety, and we were heading due east, south of Tavistock. Again Dartmoor was on our left. We were so low that we caught no glimpse of the prison, even though it stands high up on the hills. Six minutes after leaving the first target we had circumnavigated two sides of the Moor. At six and a half, we crossed the River Dart. At seven we were coming up to Ashburton and the A38, which would guide us in to our second target run.

This time the lead pair were on the right. On the map the IP looked glaringly obvious – a big interchange and bridge on the main road. But again things were not so easy from the air and at speed. It turned out that the roundabout was almost invisible from the direction of our approach. It nestled under the bank of a hill, and did not come into view until the last second. But the leader called 'Switches!' and I hit the button.

At ten seconds we crossed the River Teign, which seemed about right. Thereafter I found it impossible to identify distinct features. We were over the edge of some big woods, which seemed wrong. Then there was a round Victorian folly tower on a ridge dead ahead of us: Lawrence Castle. Something was definitely wrong. The *other* pair should have been over it. We were all a kilometre to the left of track. Too late to worry.

At forty-six seconds we banked right and climbed, to come on to the attack vector behind the leaders. For once I managed to keep my head up and my eyeballs pointing in the right direction. Up we soared in a thrilling arc. Suddenly the lead pair were sweeping back over us. They should have been well ahead, but somehow we had almost caught them up and got in beneath them.

Over went the leader, momentarily upside-down above us as he tipped in at the target. Number Two followed him into the dive. Three seconds later we too were upside-down, pulling hard left, over the top and down. Dead on our nose, the leaders hurtled down the dive like finned, grey-green bullets. Beyond them the lattice-work of the target mast showed up beautifully. Nobody could miss this one.

'In visual,' called the leader. 'Two – in visual.' 'Three – in visual.' 'Four – in visual.' Everybody had it. The ring of our sight was steady round the building at the base of the tower, our pipper buried in the building's base. In the final seconds of the attack I lost track of the aeroplanes ahead of us, unable to take my eyes off the spectacle of the target growing in the sight. Time seemed to stand still as we bored towards the ground. Then *wham!* – we pulled up as violently as if we had hit something solid, and the air came alive with satisfactory reports: 'Two – out contact.' 'Three – out contact.' 'Four – out contact.' Radio silence fell again as the two pairs reformed into defensive battle and steered 325 towards Barnstaple and home. Altogether, it had been an impressive performance, even though the students had only been following. Their turn to lead would come soon enough.

As they drew near the end of the Brawdy course, their thoughts turned more and more to the kind of aeroplane which they would be flying next. In vain the instructors, with the knowledge furnished by their own experience, assured them that they would be delighted to fly *any* fast jet to which they found themselves posted. (It is an established fact that every pilot, every squadron, becomes fiercely loyal to whatever type of aircraft he or it is flying, and cheerfully disparages all other kinds.)

Unwilling to accept this fact of life, the students stuck out vociferously for their particular fancies, and the crew-room often erupted in repartee as people ran down their comrades' choices. John McCrea, because of his preference for low-level work, had set his heart on Buccaneers. 'Bloody mud-movers!' everyone shouted. Someone else was for Jaguars. 'You realize you need reheat to get those things out of the park,' they told him. For Paul Field, it was Lightnings or bust. 'Great!' the rest of them yelled. 'Join the Historic Aircraft Section at Binbrook [the Lightning base in Lincolnshire].'

For the students to state their preferences was one thing, to achieve them was quite another, for much depended on the slots available. The uncertainties were finally resolved by a Role Disposal Board held at Gloucester, attended by Squadron Leader Johnson together with the appropriate Flight Commander.

At Brawdy a barrel of beer was laid on in the crew-room, for a celebration in the evening as soon as the postings were known. Everyone waited in an atmosphere of increasing tension for the Boss to return with the news. When he did come back he summoned the students into his office one at a time and told them their fate. Each then returned to the gallery in the crew-room.

Typically, John McCrea took his good news quietly. 'Buccaneers!' he said with a grin as he reappeared, and he sat down with a pint. Paul Field's re-entry was more ebullient. He burst into the room, struck a victorious stance with both arms up, and shouted: 'Lightnings!' The others on the course all got what they wanted – Howard Davies Jaguars, Louis McQuade Phantoms. Soon, with something definite to look forward to, they were all letting down the tension.

Yet none of them harboured any illusions. In spite of the fact that they had worked like slaves for two and a half years, and learned a prodigious amount, they knew that the road ahead still went steeply uphill.

11

To the Sharp End

John McCrea joined the Buccaneer Operational Conversion Unit at Honington in May 1981. But because the original text of this book went to press soon after that, it could not report on how he fared at the OCU or later. This final chapter therefore describes the OCU in general terms, and moves on to XV Squadron at Laarbruch, in West Germany, to which John McCrea was eventually posted.

Honington lies in the fat, soft farm land of Suffolk, just north of Bury St Edmunds. Cock pheasants strut about the boundaries of the camp, and rabbits are numerous enough to be a menace on the runways. In brewing terms this is Greene King country – a fact of some significance to RAF personnel – and draught Abbot ale is on sale in most of the local bars. Even more than other RAF bases, Honington has a look of transience. The gardens of the married quarters, though neat enough, are almost entirely down to grass. At the end of the winter the football pitches are scarcely scarred. It looks as if no one has time, or stays here long enough, to garden or play games.

The 237 OCU course now lasts only ten weeks, and its purpose is simple: to train pilots and navigators to operate the Buccaneer. For a pilot who comes straight from flying Hawks at Brawdy, it is a fundamental change to be teamed with a second crew member. (Although the Hawk does have a back seat, in the RAF version of the aeroplane it is there purely for instructional purposes.) Before they have tried it, some people dislike the idea of flying with a partner; but, in the words of Wing Commander Phil Wilkinson, Chief Instructor at Honington until the summer of 1981, 'Once they *have* tried it, they never look back. Nowadays no one fancies himself as a steely-eyed demigod in a white scarf – particularly in a Buccaneer, which is a complicated aircraft, as well as being old-fashioned. Although it's steam-driven, with very few automatic aids, it's asked to do an enormous amount, and that means both crew members have got to work very hard to get the best out of it.'

Originally commissioned by the Royal Navy, the Buccaneer was conceived as a low-level maritime strike aircraft, designed to operate from aircraft-carriers. It was therefore equipped with folding wings, a tail-hook, and a system that blows air from the engines over the wings and tail-planes during take-off and landing, thus making the aeroplane (as one pilot put it) think it is going faster than it really is. It was also built with great strength (and therefore weight), so that it could sustain the impact of the controlled crashes which carrier-landings generally amount to.

The factors which have kept it in service so long are its exceptional endurance and its excellence as a weapons-platform. It is one of the most stable fast jets in RAF service, and when expertly handled can still outperform many more modern types in its crucial, low-level role.

For a pilot used to the Hawk, one immediately obvious drawback to the Buccaneer is its poor visibility. The thick windshield pillars and canopy arches block out substantial areas of sky, and the gauges that sprout from the top of the coaming (some of them added as afterthoughts) further reduce the lookout. 'Flying in close formation, you have to crane back and forth to keep the leader in sight, because the whacking great canopy arch is blocking the very angle you want to see along,' said Wing Commander Wilkinson. 'When you're in the back seat, you can tell whether a student pilot's really keeping a lookout or not from the way he's sitting. If his head's turning but his shoulders are staying still, you know that there are quite large areas of sky which he can't see at all. To keep a proper lookout, he's got to lean right back and then right forward.'

Another peculiarity of the Buccaneer is that no training aircraft, with duplicated controls, has ever been built. A student's first flight is thus liable to be a tense occasion: although his instructor sits in the back, he is powerless to intervene, except verbally, if something starts to go wrong.

To prepare for the first sortie, the students do ten days' ground-school and fifteen hours in the simulator, learning the aeroplane's systems, and to some extent its feel. Besides full instrumentation, the simulator has a visual display projected on a television screen just outside the windshield, which effectively gives the illusion of taking off, flying at low level, and landing. The display is created by an ingenious system in which a mobile television camera tracks all over the face of a vast, vertically mounted relief map. The camera also moves in and out, towards and away from the surface of the map, thus giving the impression that the aircraft is descending or climbing.

As well as working in the simulator, the students fly two or three sorties in a specially modified, dual-control Hunter fitted with a central instrument panel exactly the same as that of the Buccaneer. Then comes the first trip in the Buccaneer itself – often, according to one instructor, the climax of the whole course in terms of excitement. 'All it proves,' he said, 'is what everyone knew all along – that the simulator is *not* like the real thing.'

The Buccaneer's normal training speed – 420 knots – is the same as that of the Hawk, and therefore what the pilots are already used to. And yet, although they have already flown extensively at 250 feet in Wales and the West Country, at the OCU they are not allowed

186

below 500 feet, except when bombing on the ranges. This is a contentious point, often raised in the past few years by the instructors and senior staff of the OCU, who believe that they should train students down to 250 feet. But they have been persistently refused permission to do so by their superiors on the grounds that it is too difficult and dangerous.

Having mastered the basic handling of the aircraft, the crew must learn to fly it accurately in formation, and this many pilots find the most difficult single skill to acquire. To judge one's position in relation to another aeroplane two or three thousand yards away, to anticipate what the other pilot is going to do next, and to preserve the geometry of a four-ship or even six-ship formation in a turn, are things that can be learned only by experience. One difficulty is that the judgement of distance is necessarily subjective: what looks to one crew like 3000 yards may seem like 2500 to another and 3500 to a third.

As at Brawdy, the training constantly emphasises that the point of maintaining precise formation is not aesthetic but practical. In Wing Commander Wilkinson's words, 'The aim is not to look pretty, but to make sure that the combined eyes of the formation can see the maximum amount of sky all round them and provide the best possible defensive cover. The radar warning receiver is a perfectly good piece of equipment, but if a fighter pilot is unreasonable enough to slip up on you with his radar switched off, you need the Mark-One eyeball working at full stretch.'

The crew's next most difficult task is to produce a really accurate approach to the target during bomb attacks. The ranges most used by the OCU are those in the Wash and up the east coast, and it is there that the students learn the Buccaneer's three basic modes of attack – lay-down, bunt, and toss.

In lay-down, the aeroplane makes a level run straight over the target and delivers its bombs without pulling up. In a bunt, or dive attack, it runs in level and then, a few seconds short of the target, pulls up to 1000 feet, tips in and bombs from a shallow dive. A bunt retard attack is one in which the bomb is slowed down by a parachute of its own, giving the aircraft more time to get out of the way.

A toss attack is a kind of lob, specially developed for the delivery of nuclear bombs, and designed so that the delivery aircraft is as far as possible from the target at the moment of impact. For this the Buccaneer runs in at 200 feet and then pulls up hard, releasing the bomb as it is climbing so that the weapon is flung upwards and forward along the flight-path by its own momentum. A bomb released at three miles' range takes some forty seconds to reach its target, and in that time the pilot puts as much distance as he can between himself and the explosion, continuing his pull-up until he goes over backwards and rolls out at about 5500 feet, pointing in the direction opposite to that of his approach.

A lay-down attack can be either visual or radar-guided. If visual, it is done almost entirely by eye. The navigator helps the pilot by dialling the wind-readings into the computer which generates his sight-picture; but the steering, run in, aiming, and bomb-release are all done by the pilot. In a radar-guided attack, by contrast, the weapon delivery is done almost entirely by the navigator.

The same is true of an automatic toss attack. The navigator uses the radar to approach the target, and the computer linked into the radar takes account of all the relevant information – speed of approach, height, speed and direction of wind, movement of target (if it is a ship) – before deciding when to release the bomb. The pilot then pulls up and over as hard as he can, goaded not only by the nature of the weapon, but also by the fact that the climb to more than 5000 feet, and the inevitable loss of speed which it entails, leave him extremely vulnerable. As soon as possible he must get back to low level.

188

Pilots coming from Brawdy, already familiar with dive attacks, must now learn to make them in the Buccaneer. First they are told to fly at 1200 feet and go into an eight-degree dive, with the navigator calling the heights as they go down, so that the pilot can keep a continuous lookout and learn what an eight-degree dive looks like in the aircraft. Then they make low-level approaches, pull up and dive.

A toss attack, because of the power of the nuclear weapon, does not need pin-point accuracy. Any error measured in hundreds of feet is acceptable. But dive and lay-down attacks do have to be flown with the greatest possible precision. Students are expected to be able to place their bombs within 140 feet of the target, and since a variation of only one degree in the pitch of the aeroplane will produce an error of over 230 feet in the fall of the bomb, they have to learn to position the aircraft with maximum accuracy.

Life on 237 OCU is much like that at any other RAF base in the United Kingdom. Instructors and students share the same crew-room, and are even more closely integrated than at Brawdy. As usual, the walls in the operational area of the Squadron are covered with admonitory, semi-humorous notices. Look out for the crop sprayer, says one. *He's spraying crops – don't crop the sprayer*. On one of the maps marking the hazards to pilots flying low up the east coast, a particular danger-spot is flagged with a sign saying *Here is an accident waiting to happen. Be careful*. There is also the inevitable Pigs' Board, on which the latest mistakes are chalked up. The entries in the slots for Prize Porker, Accused, and Charge are frequently changed as some new miscreant is pilloried, but there is one line that never alters: opposite Verdict, the entry is always Guilty.

During the ten-week course each student gets about thirty sorties, or forty hours' flying. But this is the absolute minimum that most of them need, and it is always difficult for the staff to decide how much they themselves should fly with the students and how much they should let them go alone. In theory the closest supervision can be achieved, and the most intensive tuition given, if an instructor accompanies a student – whether pilot or navigator – on every sortie. In practice, however, a system of this kind is not very successful, for it gives the student no chance to relax and – worse still – deprives him of the opportunity of flying with his real partner. He comes back from a sortie without the pleasant sense of achievement which he would have gained had he successfully flown unsupervised, and he does not pile up the hours of communal effort essential to the establishment of close teamwork. Therefore, in as many sorties as possible, the students are sent together, and afterwards they go through what happened with their instructors in a verbal debrief.

Once a fortnight a summary of their progress goes to the Chief Instructor, and anyone falling behind is given as many as possible of the spare flying hours built into the programme. Every effort is made to bring each pilot up to the necessary standard, for at the OCU there is no chance of a re-course, except if a man has missed some of the syllabus through being ill. Anyone who fails – as about ten per cent do – falls out of the fast-jet stream and can only go backwards in terms of speed, to something like the Canberra or the Hercules.

Those who pass out are fully fledged pilots and navigators: they have attained a high level of skill, and are ready for posting to operational squadrons. Yet the feeling of being students persists right to the end of the OCU course. Only when they complete it have air-crew at last come to the end of their three-year training; and no matter how well they have done, they leave Honington with a great lifting of the spirit.

Anyone familiar with RAF stations in the United Kingdom finds a drastic difference as soon as he arrives at Laarbruch. From the moment he passes the sandbagged emplacement at the entrance, and the board saying (under normal circumstances) KEEN WIND STATE GREY, everything in sight confirms that the place is on a war footing.

The base was built by the Germans during the 1950s as part of their war-reparations. Forty thousand trees were cut out of a huge pine forest, and the airfield was neatly slotted into the remaining woods for maximum camouflage. Today every building is painted a drab green that blends easily with field and forest. The aircraft of the three resident squadrons live permanently in hardened shelters scattered and tucked away among the trees, all facing in different directions so as to minimize possible bomb damage. Each squadron has a hardened PBF, or pilot briefing facility, which is its operational headquarters in war and peace, and there is a similiar facility for the crews on Quick Reaction Alert.

Surface-to-air missiles defend the base against air attack; barbed wire, fire-positions, camouflaged command posts, tracker dogs and police patrols against ground intruders. In an emergency some of the barbed-wire barriers can be moved to seal the whole airfield off, and the ground-defence communications network is encased in concrete so that it cannot be interdicted. At the ends of the runways huge heaps of crushed rock and rolls of steel mesh stand ready for instant repair-work.

A similar state of readiness exists at all four bases manned by the RAF in Germany. One, Wildenrath, houses two squadrons of Phantom air-defence fighters, of which one battle flight is permanently on QRA. Yet the greatest proportion of RAF Germany's effort goes into fulfilling its main task within NATO – the provision of a conventional and nuclear strike force for the immediate support of land operations.

At Gutersloh, the only RAF station east of the Rhine, there are two squadrons of Harriers and one of Puma helicopters. At Brüggen there are four squadrons of

Jaguar low-level fighter-bombers, and at Laarbruch two squadrons of Buccaneers, besides one of photo-reconnaissance Jaguars. Another vital element in the air-defence pattern is the deployment of Nike and Hawk ground-to-air missile battalions. All these units are part of the Second Allied Tactical Air Force, to which, besides the RAF, the air forces of Germany, Holland, Belgium and the United States all contribute.

The co-operation between the different forces is impressively close. An RAF pilot flying anywhere over West Germany, Holland or Belgium, and calling up a ground station, is immediately answered in excellent English and given all the help he needs. Most military airfields in all the countries are equipped to receive and service the other nations' aircraft and send them back into battle – and indeed a programme of exchanges between the national forces gives air and ground crews practical experience of working together. In war, the British pilot of a Phantom interceptor might easily find himself being directed by a German fighter-controller in a Luftwaffe ground-radar station who would guide the aircraft into a favourable position for a kill and then help the pilot recover to the nearest suitable airfield.

Laarbruch, just on the Dutch border, is a town in itself, with streets named in a curious combination of English and German. If 'Oxford Strasse' looks odd at first glance, 'North Circular Strasse' looks even more odd – although of course it is entirely appropriate that the medical centre should be in Harley Strasse. Altogether some 6000 people, including a number of German civilians, live and work in the camp. The place has its own school, church, NAAFI supermarket, sports fields, tennis courts, swimming pool, cinema, numerous social clubs and citizens' band radio. Yet it is not the excellent social and recreational facilities that strike a visitor most: what makes an overwhelming impact is Laarbruch's obvious readiness for war.

People on the base seem curiously reluctant to name

the enemy. Almost always they speak of 'them', 'him', 'the potential adversary' or 'the Warsaw Pact'. Hardly ever does anyone say 'the Russians'. Yet nobody is under any illusions as to where the big threat lies.

A good deal of the Squadron's energy is devoted to the unending series of evaluations that test the station's preparedness for combat. A sequence of monthly Minivals (miniature evaluations) leads up to the Maxeval, which itself is preparation for the Taceval, or tactical evaluation, the annual culmination of the training programme.

The preliminary inspections are carried out by the RAF itself, but the Taceval is sprung by a special NATO team which arrives without warning at any hour of the day or night and requires the base to move at once into its war posture. Normal life comes to a standstill. On the airfield itself call-out hooters sound the alarm. The married quarters in the nearby town of Goch also have hooters. Police vehicles circulate with sirens and loud-speakers going. Officers in private accommodation are telephoned. All ranks hurry back to base and take up their prearranged roles in the task of putting the Squadron on an operations footing.

The airfield is divided into sectors, and each sector is closed and guarded. The air-crews of each squadron move into their hardened PBF with everything they are going to need during the next few days, down to the equipment from the coffee bar. The place is already equipped with water and emergency rations for seven days, and once the big steel doors are closed, it becomes a sanctuary, a closed environment proof against anything except a direct bomb-hit, its air under positive pressure and fully filtered to prevent contamination from nuclear fallout or chemical and biological weapons.

Once the exercise has started, it continues for twenty-four hours a day until the NATO team call it off – probably for at least four days. During that period the air-crews wear their carbon-impregnated NBC

193

undersuits all the time; and if they have to go outside, they don portable respirator systems, known as AR5s – hideous black rubber hoods which pull right over the head on to chest and shoulders, claustrophobic and hot in the extreme. A clear visor enables the wearer to see, and air is blown to his face by the filter-unit which he carries round with him; even so, to wear the mask for hours on end is a severe physical and mental trial.

Anyone entering the PBF from outside must pass through an elaborate decontamination process carried out in a series of airlocks, and involving much application of Fuller's Earth (bentonite powder). Going out is a simpler process, but still tiresome. In the open, CS gas is used to make sure that people do not shirk wearing their respirators.

Throughout the exercise everything possible is done to make the scenario realistic. Intruders try to infiltrate the various sectors and attack the aeroplanes. If the DS declares an air-raid, even the air-crews inside the PBF put on their respirators and tin helmets and adopt a cowering posture, against the possibility of the building being breached and its air contaminated. If the building is declared damaged, the crew must carry out prearranged evacuation procedures, deal with the casualties, and fall back on their stand-by facilities.

Everything is based on the assumption that the war will last only a few days. After that – according to present NATO theory – either the diplomats will have taken the situation in hand and started to talk it out, or the super-powers will have resorted to all-out nuclear bombardment and blown the world to pieces. Hence the remark made by one officer in XV Squadron's PBF: 'In the event of war this building becomes our home, until it's all over or until we're no longer here.'

At the end of the exercise the NATO team assigns the base ratings, from one to four, on every aspect of its performance. If a high proportion of ones is scored, all is well; but if there are too many fours, a repeat of the whole exercise may well be called in the near future. Every Taceval is an immensely tiresome upheaval and disruption of normal flying training. Yet everyone accepts without question the necessity of holding it, for the point of maintaining a presence in Germany is to be ready for war.

It is thus hardly surprising that a new pilot, joining XV Squadron for the first time, finds himself in a tough and demanding environment. XV Squadron is one of the oldest in the RAF, having been formed at Farnborough in 1915, and it was the first unit in RAF Germany to operate Buccaneers, which it flew in from England in 1971. The hind's head which features in its crest derives from the fact that the squadron flew Hawker Hind biplane bombers during the 1930s; but the emblem is no longer borne by the unit's aeroplanes, which now carry only the number XV.

A newcomer's first day at Laarbruch is not too serious, for the Squadron has a lighthearted tradition whereby members swap roles and impersonate each other, just to confuse him. In the evening a Meet and Greet is held specially for his benefit in the officers' mess. There, together with his wife, if he has one, he is introduced to as many officers and their wives as possible. The atmosphere is informal and friendly, and he gets a foretaste of how much closer-knit this community is than the ones he has known so far.

Thereafter, the going is hard, for everything he has learned already is no more than a foundation on which he must now raise himself to an altogether higher level of skill. In the words of Wing Commander Trevor Nattrass, the officer commanding XV Squadron in 1981, 'Despite the fact that he's got his wings and graduated from the Buccaneer OCU, he's still a long way from what we would consider to be a combat-ready pilot.'

Usually he is given a mentor to monitor his progress through the training syllabus that brings him up to combat-ready status, and often he is teamed up with an experienced navigator, who can give him a great deal of help. Nor is that the only advantage of having a seasoned operator in the back seat: the navigator exercises the supervision required by the Squadron Commander, and also reports to him on how the new recruit is doing – whether he is being pushed too hard or whether he could go faster. Although there is a set syllabus, the Squadron Commander has discretionary powers which allow him to decide that certain parts of it be omitted if the trainee's progress is fast enough.

The pilot's first aim is to become 'combat-ready, strike', a status which allows him to fly strike missions, although not as the leader of any formation. Then, having progressed through the rest of his attack work-up, he becomes combat-ready as a wing-man. A reasonably competent pilot should reach combat-ready status in six months.

His next target is to become a pairs leader, and this he may achieve within a year of arriving on the Squadron; but, unless he is of exceptional ability, he is not likely to reach the coveted status of fours leader during his first three-year tour. Although a few pilots do achieve this level during their first tour, the majority must expect to wait till their second.

Meanwhile, he has also been working on his instrument flying. Most new pilots arrive on the squadron with an instrument rating known as a white card, the lowest form of classification. In effect this means that they are not allowed to fly below 400 feet on an instrument approach; and in practical terms it puts considerable restrictions on their flying. To become fully operational, they must pass the test to green standard, which allows them to fly on instruments down to 200 feet.

Apart from the live flying, the new pilot does much work in the Buccaneer simulator, where he learns, among everything else, the finer points of electronic warfare. This subject is of ever-increasing importance, for as the capability of radar defences and missile systems keeps improving, so air-crew need ever-more sophisticated warning systems and counter-measures to help them penetrate to their targets.

The Buccaneer is fitted with a radar warning receiver which enables the pilot to hear, and the navigator to hear and see, threats from enemy radar. The aircraft also has an electronic counter-measures pod slung beneath the wing which is capable of jamming enemy transmissions. In the air everything depends on the skill of the crew at recognizing threats early enough. If they detect the signal from a hostile ground-radar while they are still a couple of minutes away from it, they should have time to take evasive action successfully; but if they fail to pick out the threat from the mass of radar talk that clutters the sky of western Europe, they may easily fly into range of the surface-to-air missiles before they have detected their presence.

In the simulator the computer programme includes accurate representations of the actual signals emitted by Warsaw Pact radars, some recorded live in Europe and some taken from equipment captured in Middle Eastern countries. Thus it is possible for RAF – and indeed all NATO – crews to practise against the real thing, the threats which they will meet in the field. In the simulator, as in the aircraft itself, they train both to recognize the threat and to evade it. The RWR tells them not only the direction of the enemy radar, but also what its operator is doing: if he is searching with a normal sweep, the signal received is intermittent; but if he locks on to the aircraft, the signal increases to a loud warbling noise and a thick green strobe appears on the screen. In this field the diversity of the radar equipment used by the various members of NATO is a positive advantage. Whereas the equipment used by the Warsaw Pact nations is mostly of standard Soviet design, that of the Western countries is so various as to make recognition that much more of a problem for the enemy.

A pilot in his first year on XV Squadron can expect

to fly some twenty or twenty-two hours a month – an average of just under one sortie per flying day. A typical sortie lasts ninety minutes, but it may easily extend to two hours, and if the weather over the Continent is bad the Buccaneers often fly to the coastal ranges in the United Kingdom for bombing practice.

The standards demanded by XV Squadron are exacting. 'If the NATO requirement is that in a lay-down attack our crews are able to drop a bomb within 50 metres of the target,' said Wing Commander Nattrass, '*my* requirement is that my crews bomb within 25 metres – in other words, half the official margin of error. In terms of reaction time, we're talking about very, very small fractions of a second – less than a tenth, in fact.

'The frustration of the job is that you can go off and do everything else on the sortie perfectly, but then over the target react a fraction of a second late and end up with a 50-metre bomb. Our environment's so competitive that I have to make a note that the chap didn't have a very good sortie that day – and of course he feels bad if he doesn't get scores at half-standard.'

In making progress, the pilot is going both up and down a staircase simultaneously: upwards in terms of capability, and downwards in terms of the height at which he is cleared to fly. Each man is brought down gradually through a series of check-points. After a few sorties at a minimum of 500 feet, he has a check-ride with a qualified instructor, or with another pilot, to clear him down to 200 feet, still at normal training speeds, for weapon deliveries on the range. Then he is cleared down to 150 feet for range work.

On his initial attack-penetration sorties he learns to manoeuvre the aeroplane against a threat at a minimum of 500 feet. Then he is cleared to manoeuvre down to 250 feet. Eventually he goes out over the sea and flies at 100 feet, but only straight and level. Back up to 200 feet over the water, he starts evading. Finally, if he is to take part in Red Flag, the big autumn exercise in America, he trains down to 100 feet over land.

The pressure on the crew of flying at ultra-low level, and at speeds above 600 mph, is not easily appreciated by someone who has never experienced it. A Buccaneer's combat weight is about twenty-five tons, and, as Wing Commander Nattrass put it, 'That means an awful lot of energy going in one direction. It's difficult to point it in another direction, and very difficult to make it do precisely what you want. So you're always very conscious of the proximity of the ground.'

At any height, but at low level particularly, an enormous amount depends on close teamwork between pilot and navigator. Each relies heavily on the other. No matter how brilliant an aviator a pilot may be, he depends on the man in the back seat for help with navigation, weapon-aiming and firing, and evasion of enemy threats. Some crews talk to each other more than others, but on the whole the more experienced a crew is, the fewer the exchanges needed. As one XV Squadron navigator put it, 'The better you know the other person, the less you need say. You know what he's going to want before he asks for it. In a way it's like playing in a band: on good days the co-operation is *so* close that it's completely instinctive, and you just do everything together.'

On top of the normal flying training, there is a regular annual pattern of exercises. The Squadron usually pays at least one visit to Denmark, where it acts as the aggressor and puts pressure on the local defences by means of attack sorties. Exchange visits are made to other NATO units, often German air force bases, where RAF air and ground crews learn to operate in a new background, with different procedures, and exchange ideas on methods and tactics with their hosts.

Another annual pilgrimage is the one to Decimomannu, in Sardinia, where several of the NATO countries maintain a range for training with live weapons.

XV Squadron normally spends three weeks there, and finds the excursion valuable on many counts. One is that the weather over Capo Frasca, on the island's west coast, is almost always better than in northern Europe; another that the air-crews can concentrate on their weapon-training without the inevitable distractions that tend to break up the weeks at home. For the Squadron Commander there is the additional advantage that for three weeks he is able to export his noise from the densely populated confines of northern Germany to the uninhabited wastes of the Mediterranean – a welcome break for the Germans who, though amazingly tolerant of the noise, do nevertheless complain from time to time.

In the autumn come the major NATO exercises, on which all the flying units are co-ordinated in a full-scale war scenario, and the RAF squadrons mount sorties to support the surface armies. Yet XV Squadron's major excursion of the year is usually that to Red Flag, the big American exercise, run from Nellis Air Force Base, that takes place over the Nevada Desert.

Highly trained though they already are, the RAF crews need a special month's work-up for this exacting event. Every pilot has to be cleared down to 100 feet, and this in itself presents severe organizational problems, for scarcely anywhere in Europe is overland flying at that ultra-low level allowed. Every pilot who does train that low has to get specific individual authorization and clearance.

In the event, the RAF always finds that its rigorous preparations pay off, and that the Buccaneer crews perform extremely well against the Americans, even though the hosts' aeroplanes and equipment are more modern than our own and the exercise takes place in an unfamiliar environment. (The floor of the desert lies some 5000 feet above sea-level; the air is hot, and the sun so bright that it is often a shadow flitting across the ground which first betrays the presence of a low-flying aeroplane to interceptors waiting overhead.)

'The fact is that our tactics are very hard to counter said Wing Commander Nattrass, 'no matter who the enemy is. In the first place, at ultra-low level an aeroplane is extremely difficult to *find* – even to acquire it visually is hard. The next thing is to counter it, and that's not easy either, because at 100 feet and 600 knots we're flying very close to the limit of what is possible. A missile fired at us is just as likely to fly into the ground as it is to hit one of the aircraft. Besides, if a fighter happens to roll out behind a Buccaneer that's at 100 feet and going hard, weaving about slightly, he can't bring his guns to bear without getting very close to the turbulence. Hitting turbulence at that height is *not* a recommended pastime: it can be very disruptive of your flight-path, and if it happens to be disruptive in the wrong direction, you can give yourself a nasty fright.

'We do present the Americans with a problem. Sometimes they solve it, sometimes they don't. But they've got some excellent equipment, and they're very good at using it. So when we go to Red Flag we feel we're operating against an opponent who's better equipped, better motivated, and better trained than the potential adversary. We believe that if we can get past the Yanks, we can get past anybody.'

In Nevada all the RAF crews enjoy the freedom of being able to fly more or less anywhere unhampered by height restrictions, and to take part in Red Flag is generally a great tonic. Even so, nobody is in the least complacent. The RAF knows full well that there has recently been a quantum jump in the capability of interceptor aircraft, which the Americans have not yet fully realized. They also know that missile technology is constantly improving. As a result, they themselves are continuously looking for improvement in their own electronic counter-measures against equipment 'that's always going to be operating at the very bottom of its engagement envelope'.

*

If the RAF work hard in Germany, they do at least have compensations, among them the fact that they are extremely well placed to travel all over Europe during weekends or periods of leave. For anyone prepared to face the eight-hour drive down the Autobahn to Munich, it is perfectly possible to spend the weekend skiing in the Alps – and the Harz mountains are much closer. Paris is only four hours off by car. Amsterdam about the same. Düsseldorf is just down the road. To the east, Hamburg and Berlin are both easily accessible. Altogether, Laarbruch is an excellent spring-board for any kind of holiday excursion. Other attractions of serving there include overseas pay and duty-free drink – a bottle of whisky costing about one-third of its price in the United Kingdom.

Yet no pilot or navigator goes to Germany for its social advantages. Aircrew go there to fly, in the sharpest, toughest environment that the RAF can offer; and it is a safe bet that any fast-jet pilot posted there will find enormous satisfaction.

The officers on XV Squadron – as on all the squadrons along the Rhine – do not see themselves as heroes, ready to sacrifice themselves for their country in the event of war. Rather, they see themselves as doing a job that somebody must do: that of maintaining a credible and visibly-effective deterrent. Paradoxical as it may sound, their fundamental hope is that they will never have to fight. Their whole aim is to furnish an insurance against war – to stop war breaking out by the simple expedient of being ready for it, and being seen to be ready.

Their job is exhilarating, but also dangerous, uncomfortable, and exhausting. They do it because they consider it enormously worthwhile and believe in what they stand for. They know quite well that if war broke out many of them would never return from the sorties which they would be tasked to fly. Their wives know it too. They all accept the risk because they are convinced that somebody must shoulder the bur-

202

den of defending the West – and in shouldering it they find a satisfaction denied to many of their civilian contemporaries.

Not many people have the temperament or ability to fly as low and hard as they do. Not many people believe as strongly as they do in the rightness of their chosen profession. In their skill, in their dedication, and above all in their small numbers, today's fast-jet pilots are the true successors of The Few.

Postscript

The text for the original hardback edition of this book went to press in June 1981. Since then the six men who began training together have all moved on in different directions.

Trevor Lewis fulfilled his other ambition of going to university and took a three-year course at Reading. In June 1982 he sat his final examinations and gained a 2:2 honours degree in physics and electronics, with subsidiary mathematics.

Looking back, he felt it was a kind of miracle that he had flown at all. 'But at least I did go solo in a jet,' he said. 'To have failed without going solo would have been far worse.' Sometimes he is positively glad he failed, since his departure from the RAF gave him the chance to read for a university degree. His ambition now is to become a research scientist and 'to work on the frontiers of technology'.

He married Barbara, the girl he met while at Henlow, in September 1980.

Al Stewart at first seemed to justify the faith shown in him by Air Vice Marshal Bairsto, who sent him for navigator training when he withdrew from the pilot stream. On the standard navigators' course at Finningley he passed out second. He then went to Brawdy for familiarization training on Hawks, and by a coincidence that pleased him greatly, was posted to the

Buccaneer OCU at Honington on the same course as John McCrea.

There, however, he changed his mind yet again, and after some 40 hours withdrew from the RAF altogether, giving as his main reason the fact that he did not want to spend the rest of his working life flying around in aeroplanes. He was pleasantly surprised to find that the RAF did not put any great pressure on him to continue.

Back in civilian life, he gave chartered accountancy a brief trial, but after only three months returned to Richard Granger, the wine-merchants in Newcastle for whom he had worked before he joined up.

Now, looking back, he misses the flying, which he very much enjoyed, and keeps in touch with several of the friends he made in training. But he is relieved that he did not commit himself to a career which did not wholly engage him – even if he has strikingly confirmed the intuition of the boarding officers at Biggin Hill who originally suspected his motivation.

Robbie Low went from Valley to the Canberra OCU at Marham. But there too he was dogged by bad luck, in that he fell behind the training schedule because of a suspected stomach ulcer. At the end of the course he failed his Final Handling Test when he botched an 'asymmetric' landing – that is, a landing with one of the Canberra's two engines shut down – and the instructor had to take control in the last few seconds.

Because asymmetric landings are a critical aspect of Canberra operations the instructor had no alternative but to suspend his pupil. All the same, Low was surprised and upset not to be given a second chance. With perhaps another 10 hours of instruction, he might well have passed. But the official answer to his request for a second shot at the test was that, because of fuel shortages, no more hours were available. As he said, it seemed a ridiculous waste to chop someone on the verge of success after so much time and money had been invested in him.

Stripped of his wings, and bitterly disappointed, Low thought for a while of leaving the RAF, but then decided he liked the life too much, and went instead for navigator training at Finningley.

He married Sally, the girl he met at OCTU, in May 1981, and his wedding in Hitchin saw the exuberant reunion of many former comrades.

Rhod Smart, having been re-coursed at OCTU, passed out an officer at the second attempt. He then went for pilot training at Cranwell, but failed after seventy hours, and was sent for navigator training at Finningley. He passed out from there with his navigator's brevet in September 1981, and after a course at the Canberra OCU at Marham joined 100 Squadron, whose job is target-towing.

He realizes that he lacked the basic, inherent ability to fly, but as a navigator he has landed on his feet, finding work in the back of an aeroplane far more enjoyable than that in the front.

Martin Oxborrow went multi-engine, training on Jet-streams at Finningley before joining the Hercules OCU at Lyneham. He was then posted to 30 Squadron, and much enjoyed himself flying transport sorties all over Europe and North America. When supplying Army, Navy and Air Force exercises, he carries 'anything from people to bullets', and altogether finds the Hercules a great deal more civilized than fast jets. 'Apart from anything else, you can have coffee on the flight-deck.'

In the spring of 1982 he became heavily involved in the airlift which supplied British forces in the Falklands. By the end of the war he had made the long haul to Ascension Island twelve times: a fourteen-hour flight each way, with a brief stop in Africa, carrying every kind of stores, including what he tactfully described as 'very large bullets'.

Like all the Hercules crews involved, he operated to far higher limits than usual. In April alone he flew 92 hours – as much as he had in the previous three months. 'It's by far the busiest I've ever been,' he said, 'but morale is fantastically high.'

Happily, his marriage settled down after its difficult passage, and on 21 July Anne-Marie had her first child, Stephen.

John McCrea proved the only one of the six who passed out to become a fast-jet pilot.

He found the Buccaneer OCU at Honington 'awful,' and did not enjoy his ten-week course there at all. He did badly and came close to failing.

His main problem was the 'repressive atmosphere,' which reminded him depressingly of Linton. 'Obviously there were some very pleasant and helpful people there,' he says, 'but on the whole I found it like going back to school – a great let-down after the freedom of Brawdy.' Nevertheless, he passed out in the end, and as soon as he reached XV Squadron at Laarbruch, he found everything entirely different. 'The Squadron is superb,' he says simply. 'Not only is everything completely professional. The best feature is that even the most experienced pilots are one's close friends, rather than one's instructors and superiors, and the way they share their experience is terrific.'

In January 1982 McCrea had the bad luck to break an ankle skiing. The accident put him off flying for three months, but it had the beneficial effect of enabling him to indulge in the Squadron's social life more freely than would otherwise have been possible. He thus got to know colleagues and their families quicker than he might have. He finds the Squadron's lifestyle much to his liking: not the least advantage is that, because a posting is for at least two years, people get to know each other far better than on relatively short training courses.

His personal transport has kept pace with his own progress. He now drives a white AC 3000 ME, one of only 42 in existence. With its three-litre engine mounted transversely in the middle of its fibreglass body, the car is capable of 120 mph – which it often does on the German Autobahns.

Above all, though, it is the work that McCrea finds rewarding. 'The Buccaneer's a lovely airplane,' he says. 'Flying it is fairly hard work, and it's a real pig in the circuit. You have to give it constant attention to make it do what *you* want, rather than what *it* wants. But once you realize that and are positive with it, it becomes great fun.'

The fact that his Squadron might have to deliver nuclear weapons in the event of war does not worry him. 'It's treated as a fact of life. The atmosphere on the Squadron may appear very relaxed, but under the joviality there is a hard core of seriousness. Our job is to fight if we have to, and we aim to do the job properly.'

Acknowledgements

Without the generous and enthusiastic co-operation of the RAF as a whole, it would have been impossible to write this book. The authors would therefore like to thank all the officers and NCOs, at the training establishments and in the front-line units, who went out of their way to provide facilities and answer questions. Visitors are a nuisance at any busy RAF station; yet nowhere were we received with anything but courtesy and good humour.

Our particular thanks are due to Wing Commander Roy Bennett, himself a former fast-jet pilot, Project Officer for both the book and the BBC television series. On our behalf he travelled thousands of miles, made hundreds of contacts and arranged innumerable interviews, all with exemplary patience and diplomacy. No authors will ever find a more pleasant or efficient liaison officer.

COLIN STRONG
DUFF HART-DAVIS
August, 1982

Index

212

All Futura Books are available at your bookshop or newsagent, or can be ordered from the following address:
Futura Books, Cash Sales Department,
P.O. Box 11, Falmouth, Cornwall.

Please send cheque or postal order (no currency), and allow 45p for postage and packing for the first book plus 20p for the second book and 14p for each additional book ordered up to a maximum charge of £1.63 in U.K

Customers in Eire and B.F.P.O. please allow 45p for the first book, 20p for the second book plus 14p per copy for the next 7 books, thereafter 8p per book.

Overseas customers please allow 75p for postage and packing for the first book and 21p per copy for each additional book.